Thank you very much for reading this book.

I0084326

Title: Rebuilding Trust
Subtitle: Redemption's Echoes in a World Striving to Mend the Fabric of Trust

Series: Echoes of the Trustless Dawn: Unveiling Humanity's Journey in a World Without Faith
Author: Maxwell J. Aromano

Table of Contents

Introduction
Shattered Illusions

In a world where trust has been fractured, where illusions of safety and security lie shattered at our feet, we find ourselves at a pivotal moment in history. The fabric of trust that once bound societies together has been torn asunder by betrayals both large and small. As we stand amidst the rubble of broken promises and shattered illusions, we are confronted with a daunting question: how do we begin to rebuild what has been lost?

The journey of rebuilding trust is a multifaceted one, encompassing both individual and collective efforts to mend the bonds that have been sundered. In this introduction, we will set the stage for our exploration of trust, redemption, and the echoes of redemption that reverberate through our world.

Shattered Illusions:

In the aftermath of betrayal, the world is left reeling from the realization that the foundations upon which it was built are not as solid as once believed. Shattered illusions lie strewn across the landscape, stark reminders of the fragility of trust and the consequences of misplaced faith.

Characters grapple with the harsh reality of their shattered illusions, coming to terms with the betrayal of those they once held dear. For some, the revelation is a devastating blow, shattering their faith in humanity and leaving them adrift in a sea of uncertainty. For others, it is a wake-up call, a harsh reminder that trust must be earned, not freely given.

The emotional toll of shattered illusions is profound, affecting not only individuals but entire societies. Trust, once taken for granted, becomes a precious commodity, hoarded and guarded jealously against further betrayal. Yet amidst the pain and disillusionment, there is a glimmer of hope, a faint whisper of redemption on the horizon.

As we delve deeper into the consequences of shattered illusions, we begin to see the seeds of renewal taking root. From the ashes of betrayal, new bonds of trust begin to form, forged in the crucible of adversity and tempered by the fires of experience. It is a slow and painful process, fraught with uncertainty and doubt, but it is also a journey of hope and redemption.

In the chapters that follow, we will explore the various aspects of this journey, from the collective healing process to the role of technology in rebuilding trust. We will examine the challenges and triumphs of individuals as they navigate the rocky terrain of trust in a world scarred by betrayal. And we will reflect on the choices we must make as individuals and as a society to secure a future built on the solid foundation of trust.

But before we embark on this journey, let us take a moment to reflect on the shattered illusions that lie at the heart of our story. For it is only by confronting the harsh truths of our past that we can hope to build a better future, one grounded in trust, redemption, and the echoes of redemption that reverberate through the ages.

Seeds of Renewal

In a world where trust has been fractured, where illusions of safety and security lie shattered at our feet, we find ourselves at a pivotal moment in history. The fabric of trust that once bound societies together has been torn asunder by betrayals both large and small. As we stand amidst the rubble of broken promises and shattered illusions, we are confronted with a daunting question: how do we begin to rebuild what has been lost?

The journey of rebuilding trust is a multifaceted one, encompassing both individual and collective efforts to mend the bonds that have been sundered. In this introduction, we will set the stage for our exploration of trust, redemption, and the echoes of redemption that reverberate through our world.

Seeds of Renewal:

Amidst the devastation wrought by betrayal and shattered illusions, there lies a glimmer of hope: the seeds of renewal. Like tender shoots pushing their way through the cracks in the pavement, these seeds represent the possibility of a brighter future, one where trust is not just a distant memory but a living, breathing reality.

Characters, once paralyzed by the weight of their disillusionment, begin to find new purpose in the wake of betrayal. They channel their pain and anger into positive action, working tirelessly to rebuild what has been lost. For some, this means seeking justice for past wrongs, holding those responsible to account for their actions. For others, it means reaching out to those who have been hurt, offering a hand of friendship and support in their time of need.

The collective healing process begins in earnest as communities come together to mend the bonds that have been broken. Through acts of kindness and compassion, they begin to rebuild the trust that once held them together, forging new connections and strengthening old ones in the process. It is a slow and painstaking process, fraught with setbacks and challenges, but with each small victory, the seeds of renewal take root and begin to flourish.

Technology, once seen as a source of division and distrust, begins to emerge as a force for good in the rebuilding process. Innovations and safeguards are introduced to regain faith in the systems that govern our lives, ensuring greater transparency and accountability every step of the way. Ethical considerations are carefully weighed and debated, ensuring that technology is used not as a tool of oppression, but as a means of empowerment for all.

Individuals, too, undergo a process of renewal as they navigate the transition from a trustless to a trusting society.

They confront their fears and insecurities head-on, finding the courage to open their hearts once more to the possibility of trust and connection. It is a journey fraught with uncertainty and doubt, but with each step forward, they come closer to finding the redemption they seek.

As we delve deeper into the seeds of renewal, we begin to see the outlines of a new world taking shape. It is a world built not on the shaky foundations of deceit and betrayal, but on the solid bedrock of trust and mutual respect. It is a world where the echoes of redemption reverberate through every interaction, binding us together in a shared vision of a better tomorrow.

But the road ahead is not without its challenges. The fragile trust that has been painstakingly rebuilt is constantly threatened by forces both internal and external. Maintaining transparency and accountability in the long term requires vigilance and commitment from all parties involved. Yet, as we stand on the cusp of a new dawn, we are filled with hope and optimism for the future.

In the chapters that follow, we will explore the challenges and triumphs of rebuilding trust in a world scarred by betrayal. We will examine the role of technology in the redemption process and the ethical considerations that must be taken into account. We will delve into the personal struggles of individuals as they navigate the rocky terrain of trust in a society in transition. And we will reflect on the choices we must make as individuals and as a society to secure a future built on the solid foundation of trust.

But for now, let us take a moment to bask in the warmth of the seeds of renewal, knowing that they hold the promise of a brighter tomorrow for us all.

The Fragile Balance

In a world where trust has been fractured, where illusions of safety and security lie shattered at our feet, we find ourselves at a pivotal moment in history. The fabric of trust that once bound societies together has been torn asunder by betrayals both large and small. As we stand amidst the rubble of broken promises and shattered illusions, we are confronted with a daunting question: how do we begin to rebuild what has been lost?

The journey of rebuilding trust is a multifaceted one, encompassing both individual and collective efforts to mend the bonds that have been sundered. In this introduction, we will set the stage for our exploration of trust, redemption, and the echoes of redemption that reverberate through our world.

The Fragile Balance:

As we embark on the journey of rebuilding trust, we are acutely aware of the fragile balance that must be maintained. Like a delicate house of cards, trust can be easily toppled by the slightest misstep, threatening to undo all of the progress that has been made.

In the aftermath of betrayal, the world finds itself teetering on the brink of chaos. The wounds of the past are still raw, and the scars run deep. Yet amidst the pain and uncertainty, there is a sense of cautious optimism, a belief that perhaps, just perhaps, redemption is possible.

But redemption does not come without its challenges. The path ahead is fraught with obstacles, both seen and unseen, that threaten to derail our progress at every turn. Maintaining the fragile balance of trust requires constant vigilance and unwavering commitment from all parties involved.

Characters, once united in their quest for redemption, find themselves tested as never before. Old wounds are reopened, old grudges reignited, threatening to tear apart the fragile bonds of trust that have been painstakingly rebuilt. Yet amidst the chaos, there is also opportunity for growth and renewal, as individuals confront their demons and emerge stronger on the other side.

The collective healing process, too, is fraught with peril. As communities come together to rebuild what has been lost, they must navigate the delicate dance of forgiveness and reconciliation, balancing the need for justice with the desire for peace. It is a difficult and often painful process, but one that is necessary if trust is to be restored.

Technology, once seen as a beacon of hope in the darkness, now stands at a crossroads. On the one hand, it has the potential to revolutionize the way we rebuild trust, providing new tools and innovations to help us navigate the challenges ahead. On the other hand, it also poses new risks and challenges, as we grapple with the ethical implications of its use.

Individuals, too, find themselves walking a tightrope as they navigate the transition from a trustless to a trusting society. They must confront their own fears and insecurities, learning to let go of the past and embrace the promise of a brighter future. It is a journey filled with uncertainty and doubt, but also one filled with hope and possibility.

As we delve deeper into the fragile balance of trust, we begin to see the outlines of a new world taking shape. It is a world built not on the shaky foundations of deceit and betrayal, but on the solid bedrock of trust and mutual respect. It is a world where the echoes of redemption reverberate through every interaction, binding us together in a shared vision of a better tomorrow.

But the road ahead is long and uncertain, and the challenges we face are daunting. Yet amidst the uncertainty, there is also hope, for we know that so long as we remain committed to the journey, redemption is within our grasp. And so, with courage and determination, we set forth into the unknown, knowing that together, we can overcome any obstacle and build a future grounded in trust, redemption, and the echoes of redemption that reverberate through the ages.

Chapter 1: Aftermath of Betrayal
Explore the aftermath of betrayals in the trustless society

In the aftermath of betrayal, the fabric of society is rent asunder, leaving behind a landscape scarred by suspicion, resentment, and fear. Trust, once the cornerstone of social cohesion, lies shattered at our feet, replaced by a pervasive sense of disillusionment and betrayal. As we navigate the wreckage of our shattered illusions, we are confronted with the harsh reality of life in a trustless society.

The aftermath of betrayal is a deeply personal experience, as individuals grapple with the emotional fallout of having their trust betrayed. For many, the betrayal cuts to the very core of their identity, shaking their faith not only in the betrayer but in themselves and their ability to trust others. The emotional toll of betrayal is profound, leaving behind a trail of broken hearts and shattered dreams in its wake.

But the impact of betrayal extends far beyond the individual level, reverberating through every level of society like ripples on a pond. Communities are torn apart as trust evaporates, replaced by suspicion and paranoia. Relationships are strained to the breaking point, as friends and loved ones struggle to reconcile the betrayal with the image they once held of the betrayer. And institutions that once served as pillars of stability find themselves rocked by scandal and corruption, their authority called into question by the very people they were meant to serve.

In the trustless society, every interaction becomes fraught with uncertainty and doubt, as individuals weigh the risk of betrayal against the potential rewards of trust. The once vibrant tapestry of human connection is replaced by a cold, calculating calculus of self-preservation, as people guard their hearts against further pain and disappointment. Yet amidst the despair, there is also a glimmer of hope, as individuals begin to come to terms with the harsh realities of life in a trustless society and search for ways to rebuild what has been lost.

As we delve deeper into the aftermath of betrayal, we begin to see the contours of a society in crisis. The bonds that once held us together have been severed, replaced by a yawning chasm of distrust and suspicion. Yet amidst the wreckage, there is also the potential for renewal, as individuals and communities come together to confront the pain of betrayal and forge a path forward. It is a journey filled with uncertainty and doubt, but also one filled with hope and possibility. And as we navigate the tumultuous waters of the trustless society, we are reminded that even in the darkest of times, there is always the possibility of redemption.

Characters grapple with shattered illusions

In the aftermath of betrayal, the once-solid foundations upon which characters built their lives crumble beneath their feet, leaving behind nothing but shattered illusions and broken dreams. For many, the betrayal cuts to the very core of their identity, forcing them to confront painful truths about themselves and those they once held dear. As they grapple with the fallout of betrayal, they are forced to confront the harsh reality of life in a trustless society.

One such character is Emily, a young woman who believed wholeheartedly in the goodness of humanity until she was betrayed by her closest friend. For Emily, the betrayal is a devastating blow, shattering her illusions of trust and leaving her adrift in a sea of uncertainty. As she struggles to come to terms with the harsh reality of the world around her, she finds herself grappling with questions of identity and self-worth, unsure of who she can trust or where she belongs.

Similarly, John, a respected member of his community, finds himself reeling in the wake of betrayal by a colleague he once considered a friend. For John, the betrayal is a profound betrayal of trust, shaking his faith not only in his colleague but in the institutions he once held dear. As he grapples with the emotional fallout of the betrayal, he finds himself questioning his own judgment and his ability to trust others, unsure of who he can turn to for support or guidance.

Yet amidst the pain and disillusionment, there is also the potential for growth and renewal. As characters confront the shattered remnants of their illusions, they begin to discover hidden reserves of strength and resilience within themselves. They learn to let go of the past and embrace the possibility of a brighter future, one built not on the shaky foundations of deceit and betrayal but on the solid bedrock of trust and mutual respect.

For Emily, the journey toward healing begins with self-reflection and self-compassion. She learns to forgive herself for placing her trust in the wrong person and finds solace in the knowledge that she is not alone in her pain. With the support of friends and loved ones, she begins to rebuild her shattered sense of self, emerging stronger and more resilient than ever before.

Similarly, John finds redemption in the act of forgiveness, both for himself and for those who have wronged him. He comes to realize that holding onto anger and resentment will only poison his own soul, and that true healing can only come from letting go of the past and embracing the possibility of a brighter future. With each step forward, he finds himself drawing closer to the redemption he seeks, as he learns to trust again and open his heart to the possibility of love and connection.

As characters grapple with their shattered illusions, they begin to see the world in a new light, one filled with hope and possibility. They come to realize that while betrayal may have shaken their faith in humanity, it has also provided them with an opportunity for growth and renewal. And as they journey toward healing, they are reminded that even in the darkest of times, there is always the possibility of redemption.

Examine the emotional toll on individuals and society

In the aftermath of betrayal, the emotional landscape of both individuals and society undergoes a profound transformation, as the bonds of trust that once held them together are shattered into a million jagged pieces. The emotional toll of betrayal is vast and far-reaching, affecting not only those directly involved but also the broader community in which they reside.

For individuals, the emotional fallout of betrayal is immediate and visceral, as they grapple with feelings of anger, sadness, and betrayal. The sense of betrayal cuts to the very core of their identity, leaving them questioning not only the motives of the betrayer but also their own judgment and self-worth. They may experience feelings of shame and self-blame, wondering what they could have done differently to prevent the betrayal from occurring.

These emotions can be overwhelming, threatening to consume individuals in a maelstrom of pain and despair. They may struggle to sleep, eat, or concentrate, as they are haunted by the specter of betrayal at every turn. Relationships may suffer as individuals withdraw from those they once held dear, fearing that they too may be capable of betrayal. Trust, once freely given, becomes a precious commodity, hoarded and guarded against further harm.

Yet amidst the pain and despair, there is also the potential for growth and renewal. As individuals confront the emotional fallout of betrayal, they begin to discover hidden reservoirs of strength and resilience within themselves. They learn to lean on friends and loved ones for support, finding solace in the knowledge that they are not alone in their pain. With each passing day, they find themselves drawing closer to healing, as they come to terms with the harsh realities of life in a trustless society and begin to rebuild what has been lost.

But the emotional toll of betrayal is not limited to individuals alone. It also reverberates through the broader community, leaving behind a trail of devastation in its wake. Trust, once the glue that held society together, is replaced by suspicion and paranoia, as individuals retreat into their own private worlds, fearing that they too may be the next victim of betrayal. Social bonds are strained to the breaking point, as friends and neighbors turn on one another in their search for someone to blame.

Communities that once thrived are torn apart by scandal and infighting, as trust in the institutions that govern them evaporates. Political leaders, once held in high esteem, find themselves besieged by accusations of corruption and malfeasance, as the public loses faith in their ability to lead. The very fabric of society is rent asunder, leaving behind a fractured landscape of distrust and uncertainty.

Yet amidst the chaos, there is also the potential for renewal. As communities come together to confront the pain of betrayal, they begin to discover new ways of relating to one another, built not on the shaky foundations of deceit and betrayal but on the solid bedrock of trust and mutual respect. They learn to listen to one another with empathy and compassion, recognizing that the only way forward is together.

In the chapters that follow, we will explore the various ways in which individuals and society grapple with the emotional toll of betrayal. We will delve into the personal struggles of characters as they come to terms with the harsh realities of life in a trustless society, and we will examine the broader impact of betrayal on the fabric of society as a whole. And through it all, we will seek to uncover the seeds of hope and redemption that lie buried beneath the rubble of broken trust, waiting to be nurtured back to life.

Foreshadow the journey toward rebuilding trust

As the dust settles on the aftermath of betrayal, a glimmer of hope begins to emerge amidst the wreckage. Though trust lies shattered and broken, there is a sense that perhaps, just perhaps, it can be rebuilt. Characters, still reeling from the emotional fallout of betrayal, begin to tentatively contemplate the possibility of a brighter future, one built on the solid foundation of trust and mutual respect.

For some, the journey toward rebuilding trust begins with a simple act of forgiveness. Though the wounds of betrayal may still be raw, they recognize that holding onto anger and resentment will only poison their own souls. They choose instead to let go of the past and embrace the possibility of a new beginning, one free from the shackles of betrayal.

Others find solace in the knowledge that they are not alone in their pain. They lean on friends and loved ones for support, finding strength in the knowledge that they are not alone in their struggle. Together, they begin to envision a world where trust is not just a distant memory but a living, breathing reality, and they set out on a journey to make that vision a reality.

Yet amidst the glimmers of hope, there are also shadows of doubt and uncertainty. Rebuilding trust is no easy task, and the road ahead is fraught with obstacles both seen and unseen. Characters must confront their own fears and insecurities, learning to trust again in a world where betrayal lurks around every corner. They must also navigate the complexities of rebuilding trust on a societal level, confronting the legacy of mistrust and suspicion that has come to define their world.

But despite the challenges that lie ahead, there is also a sense of determination and resolve. Characters refuse to be defined by the betrayals of their past, choosing instead to forge a new path forward, one guided by hope and optimism rather than fear and mistrust. They recognize that rebuilding trust will not happen overnight, but they are willing to put in the hard work and dedication required to make it a reality.

As they set out on their journey toward rebuilding trust, characters begin to lay the groundwork for a brighter future. They seek out opportunities for reconciliation and forgiveness, reaching out to those they have wronged or been wronged by in the past. They also work to rebuild the institutions and systems that have been damaged by betrayal, introducing new safeguards and measures to ensure greater transparency and accountability.

Yet amidst the optimism, there is also a sense of caution and wariness. Characters know that rebuilding trust is a delicate process, one that can easily be derailed by further betrayal or mistrust. They are acutely aware of the fragility of the trust they seek to rebuild, and they tread carefully, mindful of the pitfalls that lie ahead.

Over the course of the upcoming chapters, we will explore the various stages of the journey toward rebuilding trust, from the initial glimmers of hope to the hard-won victories and inevitable setbacks. We will delve into the personal struggles of characters as they confront their own fears and insecurities, and we will examine the broader societal implications of their efforts. And through it all, we will seek to uncover the seeds of hope and redemption that lie buried beneath the rubble of broken trust, waiting to be nurtured back to life.

Chapter 2: Societal Healing

Examine the collective healing process post-betrayal

In the aftermath of betrayal, societies are left reeling from the shockwaves of mistrust and suspicion that reverberate through their ranks. Yet amidst the chaos and uncertainty, there is also the potential for renewal and growth. As communities come together to confront the pain of betrayal, they embark on a collective healing process that seeks to mend the bonds that have been broken and forge a path toward a brighter future.

The collective healing process begins with a recognition of the shared trauma that binds individuals together. Communities gather to mourn the loss of trust and innocence that betrayal has wrought, coming together in solidarity to support one another through the darkest of times. They hold vigils and memorials to honor those who have been harmed by betrayal, acknowledging the pain and suffering that they have endured.

Yet amidst the grief, there is also the potential for solidarity and unity. As communities come together to confront the pain of betrayal, they begin to discover new ways of relating to one another, built not on the shaky foundations of deceit and betrayal but on the solid bedrock of trust and mutual respect. They learn to listen to one another with empathy and compassion, recognizing that the only way forward is together.

The collective healing process also involves a reckoning with the past, as communities confront the legacy of mistrust and suspicion that has come to define their world. They hold truth and reconciliation hearings to uncover the full extent of the betrayal that has occurred, allowing those who have been harmed to share their stories and seek closure. They also work to address the systemic issues that have allowed betrayal to flourish, introducing new safeguards and measures to ensure greater transparency and accountability in the future.

But perhaps the most important aspect of the collective healing process is the cultivation of empathy and understanding. As communities come together to confront the pain of betrayal, they begin to see one another not as enemies or adversaries, but as fellow human beings struggling to make sense of a world gone awry. They learn to recognize the humanity in one another, and in doing so, they begin to rebuild the bonds of trust that have been severed by betrayal.

The collective healing process is not easy, and it is not without its challenges. There will inevitably be setbacks and obstacles along the way, as communities grapple with the pain and trauma of betrayal. Yet amidst the darkness, there is also the potential for light, as communities come together to forge a new path forward, one built on the solid foundation of trust and mutual respect.

Throughout the following chapters, we will explore the various stages of the collective healing process, from the initial stages of mourning and grief to the eventual triumph of solidarity and unity. We will delve into the personal struggles of individuals as they come to terms with the pain of betrayal, and we will examine the broader societal implications of their efforts. And through it all, we will seek to uncover the seeds of hope and redemption that lie buried beneath the rubble of broken trust, waiting to be nurtured back to life.

Characters participate in societal recovery efforts

In the wake of betrayal, characters find themselves thrust into the heart of societal recovery efforts, grappling with the monumental task of rebuilding trust and healing the wounds that have been inflicted upon their communities. As they confront the pain and trauma of betrayal, they are called upon to step forward and play an active role in the collective healing process, contributing their skills, talents, and compassion to the task at hand.

One such character is Sarah, a community organizer with a passion for social justice. In the aftermath of betrayal, Sarah throws herself into the work of rebuilding trust and fostering solidarity within her community. She organizes neighborhood meetings and community forums to provide a space for people to come together and share their experiences, offering support and solidarity to those who have been harmed by betrayal. Through her tireless efforts, Sarah helps to create a sense of belonging and unity within her community, laying the groundwork for healing and reconciliation.

Similarly, John, a local business owner, finds himself drawn into the fold of societal recovery efforts as he grapples with the fallout of betrayal. Recognizing the importance of economic stability in rebuilding trust within his community,

John works tirelessly to support local businesses and entrepreneurs, providing resources and assistance to help them weather the storm of uncertainty. Through his efforts, John helps to rebuild the economic foundation of his community, fostering a sense of resilience and hope amidst the chaos of betrayal.

As characters like Sarah and John participate in societal recovery efforts, they begin to discover new ways of relating to one another, built not on the shaky foundations of deceit and betrayal but on the solid bedrock of trust and mutual respect. They learn to listen to one another with empathy and compassion, recognizing that the only way forward is together. Through their collective efforts, they begin to rebuild the bonds of trust that have been severed by betrayal, forging a path toward a brighter future for themselves and their communities.

Yet the road to societal healing is not without its challenges. As characters grapple with the pain and trauma of betrayal, they must also confront the legacy of mistrust and suspicion that has come to define their world. They encounter resistance and opposition from those who are reluctant to let go of the past, clinging to their anger and resentment like a security blanket. Yet characters like Sarah and John refuse to be deterred by the naysayers, pressing forward with determination and resolve in their quest to rebuild trust and heal their communities.

In the face of adversity, characters draw strength from one another, finding solace and support in the bonds of friendship and solidarity that they have forged. They come together to mourn the loss of trust and innocence that betrayal has wrought, but they also come together to celebrate the resilience and courage that have carried them through the darkest of times. Through their collective efforts, they begin to rebuild the fabric of trust that binds their communities together, laying the groundwork for a brighter future for themselves and their loved ones.

In the subsequent chapters, we will continue to explore the various ways in which characters participate in societal recovery efforts, from organizing community events to providing support and assistance to those in need. We will delve into the personal struggles and triumphs of individuals as they confront the pain and trauma of betrayal, and we will examine the broader societal implications of their efforts. And through it all, we will seek to uncover the seeds of hope and redemption that lie buried beneath the rubble of broken trust, waiting to be nurtured back to life.

Explore the role of transparency and accountability in rebuilding trust

In the aftermath of betrayal, one of the most critical components of societal healing is the establishment of transparency and accountability mechanisms. These mechanisms serve as the foundation upon which trust can be rebuilt, providing reassurance to individuals and communities that the mistakes of the past will not be repeated and that justice will be served.

Transparency begins with a commitment to openness and honesty in all aspects of governance and decision-making. It requires leaders to be forthcoming with information, sharing both their successes and their failures with the public. Transparency also means creating channels for communication and feedback, allowing individuals to voice their concerns and hold leaders accountable for their actions.

Accountability, on the other hand, is about holding individuals and institutions responsible for their actions and ensuring that they are held to the highest standards of integrity and ethics. It requires the establishment of clear guidelines and standards of conduct, as well as mechanisms for enforcing those standards and holding wrongdoers accountable for their actions.

One character who plays a pivotal role in promoting transparency and accountability is David, a journalist with a passion for uncovering the truth. In the aftermath of betrayal, David throws himself into the task of investigating the root causes of the betrayal and holding those responsible to account for their actions. Through his investigative reporting, he shines a light on the dark corners of society, exposing corruption and malfeasance wherever it may be found.

Similarly, Sarah, the community organizer, works tirelessly to promote transparency and accountability within her community. She advocates for the establishment of community oversight committees and watchdog groups, tasked with monitoring the actions of local leaders and holding them accountable for their decisions. Through her efforts, Sarah helps to create a culture of transparency and accountability within her community, ensuring that the mistakes of the past are not repeated in the future.

Yet transparency and accountability are not just the responsibility of individuals; they are also the responsibility of institutions and systems. Governments, businesses, and other organizations must take proactive steps to promote transparency and accountability within their ranks, establishing clear guidelines and procedures for reporting misconduct and ensuring that wrongdoers are held to account for their actions.

Technology also plays a crucial role in promoting transparency and accountability in the rebuilding process. From blockchain technology to ensure the integrity of financial transactions to whistleblower hotlines to report instances of wrongdoing, technology provides powerful tools for promoting transparency and holding individuals and institutions accountable for their actions.

But perhaps the most important aspect of transparency and accountability is the trust that it engenders within communities. When individuals and institutions are open and honest about their actions and decisions, it fosters a sense of trust and confidence among the people they serve. It sends a clear message that they are committed to doing the right thing, even when no one is watching.

Across the ensuing chapters, we will continue to explore the role of transparency and accountability in rebuilding trust, from the establishment of clear guidelines and standards of conduct to the use of technology to promote transparency and accountability. We will delve into the personal struggles and triumphs of individuals as they confront the challenges of promoting transparency and accountability in the aftermath of betrayal, and we will examine the broader societal implications of their efforts. And through it all, we will seek to uncover the seeds of hope and redemption that lie buried beneath the rubble of broken trust, waiting to be nurtured back to life.

Illustrate the challenges and triumphs in healing the societal wounds

In the aftermath of betrayal, healing the wounds inflicted upon society is a daunting task, fraught with challenges and obstacles at every turn. Yet amidst the darkness, there are also moments of triumph and resilience, as communities come together to confront the pain and trauma of betrayal and forge a path toward a brighter future.

One of the greatest challenges in healing societal wounds is the sheer magnitude of the task at hand. Betrayal has a way of shaking the very foundations of society, leaving behind a trail of devastation in its wake. Trust, once the cornerstone of social cohesion, lies shattered and broken, replaced by suspicion and paranoia. Rebuilding trust requires a Herculean effort, as communities must confront the legacy of mistrust and suspicion that has come to define their world.

Another challenge is the deep-seated nature of the wounds inflicted by betrayal. Betrayal cuts to the very core of our humanity, leaving behind scars that may never fully heal. The emotional toll of betrayal is profound, leaving individuals and communities reeling from the shockwaves of mistrust and suspicion that reverberate through their ranks. Healing these wounds requires not only time and patience but also a willingness to confront the pain and trauma head-on.

Yet despite the challenges that lie ahead, there are also moments of triumph and resilience as communities come together to confront the pain of betrayal. One such triumph is the emergence of solidarity and unity in the face of adversity. In the aftermath of betrayal, communities rally together to support one another, offering a shoulder to lean on and a listening ear to those in need. Through acts of kindness and compassion, they begin to rebuild the bonds of trust that have been severed by betrayal, forging a path toward healing and reconciliation.

Another triumph is the resilience of the human spirit in the face of adversity. Despite the pain and trauma of betrayal, individuals and communities refuse to be defined by their pasts. They draw strength from one another, finding solace and support in the bonds of friendship and solidarity that they have forged. Through acts of courage and determination, they begin to rebuild their lives and their communities, laying the groundwork for a brighter future for themselves and their loved ones.

Yet perhaps the greatest triumph of all is the realization that even in the darkest of times, there is always the possibility of redemption. Betrayal may have shaken our faith in humanity, but it has also provided us with an opportunity for growth and renewal. As communities come together to confront the pain and trauma of betrayal, they begin to discover new ways of relating to one another, built not on the shaky foundations of deceit and betrayal but on the solid bedrock of trust and mutual respect. And through their collective efforts, they begin to uncover the seeds of hope and redemption that lie buried beneath the rubble of broken trust, waiting to be nurtured back to life.

In the forthcoming chapters, we will continue to explore the challenges and triumphs in healing the societal wounds inflicted by betrayal. We will delve into the personal struggles and triumphs of individuals as they confront the pain and trauma of betrayal, and we will examine the broader societal implications of their efforts. And through it all, we will seek to uncover the seeds of hope and redemption that lie buried beneath the rubble of broken trust, waiting to be nurtured back to life.

Chapter 3: Technological Redemption
Explore the potential for technological redemption

In the aftermath of betrayal, technology emerges as both a tool of oppression and a beacon of hope. While it has been used to facilitate deceit and manipulation, it also holds the potential for redemption, offering innovative solutions to rebuild trust and foster transparency in society.

One avenue for technological redemption lies in the realm of blockchain technology. Blockchain, a decentralized ledger system, offers a transparent and immutable record of transactions, making it inherently resistant to tampering and fraud. By leveraging blockchain technology, societies can create a more transparent and accountable system of governance, where every transaction is recorded and verified by a network of users.

For example, blockchain technology can be used to ensure the integrity of elections, providing a secure and transparent platform for voters to cast their ballots. By recording each vote on the blockchain, societies can create a verifiable record of election results, reducing the risk of fraud and manipulation. This not only restores trust in the electoral process but also strengthens the democratic foundation of society.

Blockchain technology can also be used to promote transparency and accountability in financial transactions. By recording every financial transaction on the blockchain, societies can create a transparent and auditable record of financial activity, making it more difficult for individuals and institutions to engage in corruption or embezzlement. This not only protects the integrity of the financial system but also fosters trust and confidence among investors and consumers.

Another avenue for technological redemption lies in the realm of artificial intelligence (AI). AI has the potential to revolutionize the way we detect and prevent fraud, by analyzing vast amounts of data to identify patterns and anomalies that may indicate suspicious activity. By leveraging AI-powered algorithms, societies can create more robust systems for detecting and preventing fraud, reducing the risk of betrayal and deception.

For example, AI-powered fraud detection systems can analyze transaction data in real-time to identify potentially fraudulent activity, flagging suspicious transactions for further investigation. This not only helps to prevent financial losses but also deters would-be fraudsters from engaging in criminal activity, knowing that they are being watched by vigilant AI systems.

AI can also be used to enhance cybersecurity, by detecting and mitigating cyber threats before they have the chance to wreak havoc. By analyzing network traffic and identifying potential vulnerabilities, AI-powered cybersecurity systems can help to prevent data breaches and protect sensitive information from falling into the wrong hands. This not only safeguards the integrity of the digital infrastructure but also protects the privacy and security of individuals and organizations.

Yet perhaps the most promising avenue for technological redemption lies in the realm of decentralized technologies such as decentralized autonomous organizations (DAOs). DAOs are organizations that are governed by smart contracts, which are self-executing contracts with the terms of the agreement directly written into code. By removing the need for centralized intermediaries, DAOs offer a more transparent and democratic form of governance, where decisions are made collectively by the members of the organization.

For example, DAOs can be used to create decentralized social networks, where users have full control over their own data and can participate in the governance of the platform. By leveraging blockchain technology and smart contracts, decentralized social networks can ensure that user data is secure and private, free from the prying eyes of advertisers and third-party intermediaries. This not only restores trust in social media platforms but also empowers users to take control of their own digital identities.

Throughout the pages ahead, we will continue to explore the potential for technological redemption, from blockchain technology to artificial intelligence to decentralized autonomous organizations. We will delve into the challenges and opportunities presented by these technologies, and we will examine their potential to rebuild trust and foster transparency in society. And through it all, we will seek to uncover the seeds of hope and redemption that lie buried within the ever-evolving landscape of technology, waiting to be nurtured back to life.

Characters strive to redeem technology's role in trust

In the aftermath of betrayal, characters find themselves grappling with the role that technology played in facilitating deceit and manipulation. Yet amidst the wreckage, there is also a glimmer of hope, as characters strive to harness the power of technology for good and redeem its tarnished reputation in the eyes of society.

One such character is Dr. Maria Chen, a brilliant computer scientist who has dedicated her life to advancing the field of artificial intelligence (AI). In the wake of betrayal, Dr. Chen is haunted by the realization that the AI algorithms she helped to create were used to perpetrate acts of deception and fraud. Determined to make amends for her unwitting role in the betrayal, Dr. Chen sets out to develop AI-powered tools for detecting and preventing fraud, leveraging her expertise to create a more trustworthy and transparent digital ecosystem.

Through her tireless efforts, Dr. Chen develops an AI-powered fraud detection system that analyzes vast amounts of data to identify patterns and anomalies that may indicate suspicious activity. By leveraging machine learning algorithms, the system is able to adapt and evolve over time, becoming increasingly adept at detecting new and emerging forms of fraud. Dr. Chen's system is hailed as a groundbreaking innovation, offering hope for a future where technology can be used to promote trust and accountability in society.

Similarly, John Smith, a former software engineer turned whistleblower, finds himself at the forefront of the fight to redeem technology's role in trust. In the aftermath of betrayal, John is wracked with guilt over his complicity in the creation of surveillance tools that were used to spy on innocent civilians. Determined to atone for his past mistakes, John begins working with advocacy groups and civil liberties organizations to push for greater transparency and accountability in the tech industry.

Through his advocacy work, John helps to shine a light on the dark underbelly of the tech industry, exposing the ways in which technology has been weaponized against ordinary people. He calls for greater regulation and oversight of the tech industry, urging lawmakers to take action to protect the privacy and security of individuals in the digital age. Though his efforts are met with resistance from powerful corporate interests, John refuses to back down, knowing that the stakes are too high to ignore.

As Dr. Chen and John work tirelessly to redeem technology's role in trust, they encounter both triumphs and setbacks along the way. They face opposition from entrenched interests who seek to maintain the status quo, as well as technical challenges that threaten to derail their efforts. Yet despite the obstacles they face, they remain steadfast in their commitment to building a more trustworthy and transparent digital future.

Their efforts do not go unnoticed, as they inspire others to join the fight for technological redemption. From grassroots activists to tech industry insiders, a growing movement emerges to demand greater accountability and responsibility from those who wield power in the digital realm. Together, they work to ensure that technology is used not as a tool of oppression, but as a force for good in the world.

In the following sections, we will continue to explore the efforts of characters like Dr. Chen and John as they strive to redeem technology's role in trust. We will delve into the challenges they face and the triumphs they achieve along the way, and we will examine the broader societal implications of their efforts. And through it all, we will seek to uncover the seeds of hope and redemption that lie buried within the ever-evolving landscape of technology, waiting to be nurtured back to life.

Examine innovations and safeguards introduced to regain faith

In the aftermath of betrayal, society finds itself at a crossroads, grappling with the implications of technological advancements that were once heralded as signs of progress. Yet amidst the chaos and uncertainty, there is also the potential for redemption, as innovators and thinkers come together to develop new technologies and safeguards aimed at restoring faith in the digital world.

One of the most promising innovations in the quest for technological redemption is the development of decentralized technologies such as blockchain. Blockchain, a decentralized ledger system, offers a transparent and immutable record of transactions, making it inherently resistant to tampering and fraud. By leveraging blockchain technology, societies can create a more transparent and accountable system of governance, where every transaction is recorded and verified by a network of users.

For example, governments around the world are exploring the use of blockchain technology to ensure the integrity of elections. By recording each vote on the blockchain, societies can create a verifiable record of election results, reducing the risk of fraud and manipulation. This not only restores trust in the electoral process but also strengthens the democratic foundation of society.

Blockchain technology can also be used to promote transparency and accountability in financial transactions. By recording every financial transaction on the blockchain, societies can create a transparent and auditable record of financial activity, making it more difficult for individuals and institutions to engage in corruption or embezzlement. This not only protects the integrity of the financial system but also fosters trust and confidence among investors and consumers.

Another innovation in the quest for technological redemption is the development of artificial intelligence (AI) tools for detecting and preventing fraud. AI has the potential to revolutionize the way we detect and prevent fraud, by analyzing vast amounts of data to identify patterns and anomalies that may indicate suspicious activity. By leveraging AI-powered algorithms, societies can create more robust systems for detecting and preventing fraud, reducing the risk of betrayal and deception.

For example, AI-powered fraud detection systems can analyze transaction data in real-time to identify potentially fraudulent activity, flagging suspicious transactions for further investigation. This not only helps to prevent financial losses but also deters would-be fraudsters from engaging in criminal activity, knowing that they are being watched by vigilant AI systems.

AI can also be used to enhance cybersecurity, by detecting and mitigating cyber threats before they have the chance to wreak havoc. By analyzing network traffic and identifying potential vulnerabilities, AI-powered cybersecurity systems can help to prevent data breaches and protect sensitive information from falling into the wrong hands. This not only safeguards the integrity of the digital infrastructure but also protects the privacy and security of individuals and organizations.

Yet perhaps the most promising innovation in the quest for technological redemption is the development of decentralized autonomous organizations (DAOs). DAOs are organizations that are governed by smart contracts, which are self-executing contracts with the terms of the agreement directly written into code. By removing the need for centralized intermediaries, DAOs offer a more transparent and democratic form of governance, where decisions are made collectively by the members of the organization.

For example, DAOs can be used to create decentralized social networks, where users have full control over their own data and can participate in the governance of the platform. By leveraging blockchain technology and smart contracts, decentralized social networks can ensure that user data is secure and private, free from the prying eyes of advertisers and third-party intermediaries. This not only restores trust in social media platforms but also empowers users to take control of their own digital identities.

Over the upcoming chapters, we will continue to explore the innovations and safeguards introduced to regain faith in technology, from blockchain technology to artificial intelligence to decentralized autonomous organizations. We will delve into the challenges and opportunities presented by these technologies, and we will examine their potential to rebuild trust and foster transparency in society. And through it all, we will seek to uncover the seeds of hope and redemption that lie buried within the ever-evolving landscape of technology, waiting to be nurtured back to life.

Illustrate the ethical considerations in the technological rebuilding process

In the quest for technological redemption, characters are confronted with a myriad of ethical considerations that must be carefully navigated. As they strive to rebuild trust and foster transparency in society, they are forced to grapple with complex moral dilemmas and ethical quandaries that have far-reaching implications for the future of humanity.

One of the primary ethical considerations in the technological rebuilding process is the issue of privacy and surveillance. In the aftermath of betrayal, individuals and communities are understandably wary of invasive surveillance practices that threaten their privacy and autonomy. Characters must wrestle with the tension between security and privacy, balancing the need for surveillance to prevent fraud and deception with the fundamental right to privacy and freedom from surveillance.

For example, Dr. Maria Chen, the computer scientist, faces difficult choices as she develops AI-powered tools for detecting and preventing fraud. On the one hand, she recognizes the importance of surveillance in identifying suspicious activity and preventing fraud before it occurs. On the other hand, she is acutely aware of the potential for abuse and misuse of surveillance technologies, particularly in the hands of authoritarian regimes or unscrupulous actors.

To address this ethical dilemma, Dr. Chen works to design her fraud detection system in a way that prioritizes privacy and transparency. She incorporates robust encryption and anonymization techniques to protect sensitive data, ensuring that individuals' privacy rights are respected while still allowing for effective fraud detection. She also advocates for greater transparency and oversight of surveillance practices, calling for clear guidelines and regulations to govern the use of surveillance technologies.

Another ethical consideration in the technological rebuilding process is the issue of algorithmic bias and discrimination. As AI and machine learning algorithms become increasingly prevalent in society, there is growing concern about the potential for these algorithms to perpetuate and exacerbate existing biases and inequalities. Characters must confront the ethical implications of algorithmic bias, grappling with questions of fairness, accountability, and social justice.

For example, John Smith, the whistleblower turned advocate, is troubled by the realization that the surveillance tools he helped to create were used to target marginalized communities and perpetuate systemic discrimination.

Determined to address this injustice, he becomes a vocal advocate for algorithmic fairness and accountability, calling for greater transparency and oversight of AI algorithms to ensure that they do not perpetuate bias or discrimination.

To address the issue of algorithmic bias, John works with advocacy groups and tech industry insiders to develop guidelines and best practices for mitigating bias in AI algorithms. He calls for greater diversity and inclusion in the development process, advocating for the inclusion of diverse perspectives and lived experiences to help identify and mitigate bias in algorithmic decision-making. He also pushes for greater transparency and accountability in the deployment of AI algorithms, calling for regular audits and assessments to ensure that algorithms are fair and equitable in their outcomes.

Yet another ethical consideration in the technological rebuilding process is the issue of accountability and responsibility. As technology becomes increasingly intertwined with every aspect of society, there is a growing need for clear guidelines and mechanisms for holding individuals and institutions accountable for their actions. Characters must confront the ethical implications of accountability, grappling with questions of culpability, liability, and justice.

For example, Sarah, the community organizer, finds herself embroiled in a controversy when a data breach exposes sensitive information about members of her community. Though Sarah was not directly responsible for the breach, she feels a deep sense of responsibility to the individuals affected and is determined to ensure that those responsible are held accountable for their actions.

To address the issue of accountability, Sarah works with legal experts and advocacy groups to develop guidelines and regulations for data protection and privacy. She advocates for greater transparency and oversight of data collection and storage practices, calling for clear guidelines and regulations to govern the use of personal data. She also pushes for greater accountability for data breaches, calling for stringent penalties for individuals and institutions that fail to protect sensitive information.

In the chapters ahead, we will continue to explore the ethical considerations in the technological rebuilding process, from privacy and surveillance to algorithmic bias and discrimination to accountability and responsibility. We will delve into the challenges and dilemmas faced by characters as they navigate these ethical minefields, and we will examine the broader societal implications of their efforts. And through it all, we will seek to uncover the seeds of hope and redemption that lie buried within the ever-evolving landscape of technology, waiting to be nurtured back to life.

Chapter 4: Individuals in Transition
Characters navigate personal transitions in the rebuilding phase

In the aftermath of betrayal, individuals find themselves thrust into a period of profound transition, as they grapple with the emotional and psychological fallout of betrayal and seek to rebuild their lives in the wake of devastation. For many characters, the rebuilding phase represents a journey of self-discovery and transformation, as they confront their pasts, confront their demons, and emerge stronger and more resilient than ever before.

One such character is Emily, a young woman who was betrayed by her closest friend and confidante. In the aftermath of the betrayal, Emily finds herself adrift, struggling to make sense of the shattered pieces of her life. Yet amidst the chaos, she discovers an inner strength and resilience that she never knew she possessed. With the support of her loved ones and the guidance of a therapist, Emily begins to confront her pain and trauma head-on, embarking on a journey of self-discovery and healing.

As Emily navigates the rebuilding phase, she confronts a myriad of challenges and obstacles along the way. She grapples with feelings of anger and resentment towards her betrayer, struggling to find forgiveness and closure in the face of betrayal. Yet through therapy and introspection, she begins to understand that forgiveness is not about absolving her betrayer of responsibility, but about freeing herself from the burden of anger and resentment.

Emily also faces challenges in rebuilding her sense of trust and self-worth in the aftermath of betrayal. She struggles to open herself up to new relationships and experiences, fearing that she will only be betrayed again. Yet with time and patience, she begins to rebuild her trust in herself and others, learning to recognize her own inherent worth and value.

Another character navigating personal transitions in the rebuilding phase is Alex, a businessman who was betrayed by his colleagues and business partners. In the aftermath of the betrayal, Alex finds himself questioning everything he thought he knew about himself and his career. Yet amidst the uncertainty, he discovers an opportunity for reinvention and renewal.

As Alex embarks on a new chapter in his life, he confronts the challenge of redefining his sense of identity and purpose. He grapples with feelings of shame and inadequacy, struggling to come to terms with the fact that he was deceived by those he trusted most. Yet through introspection and self-reflection, he begins to see that his worth is not defined by his past mistakes, but by his ability to learn and grow from them.

Alex also faces challenges in rebuilding his professional reputation and rebuilding trust in his career. He struggles to regain the trust of his clients and colleagues, fearing that his past betrayal will forever tarnish his reputation. Yet with perseverance and determination, he begins to rebuild his career from the ground up, earning back the trust and respect of those around him through hard work and dedication.

As we progress through the chapters, we will continue to explore the personal transitions and transformations of characters in the rebuilding phase. We will delve into the challenges and triumphs they face as they confront their pain and trauma head-on, and we will examine the broader implications of their journeys for society as a whole. And through it all, we will seek to uncover the seeds of hope and redemption that lie buried within the hearts of individuals, waiting to be nurtured back to life.

Examine the impact of regained trust on personal relationships

In the aftermath of betrayal, the fabric of personal relationships is often torn asunder, leaving behind a trail of pain and mistrust. Yet as individuals embark on the journey of rebuilding trust, they also have the opportunity to rebuild and strengthen their personal relationships, forging deeper connections built on a foundation of honesty, transparency, and mutual respect.

One of the most profound impacts of regained trust on personal relationships is the restoration of intimacy and closeness. Betrayal has a way of erecting walls between individuals, making it difficult to truly open up and connect with one another. Yet as trust is rebuilt, these walls begin to crumble, allowing individuals to let down their guard and be vulnerable with one another once again.

For example, Sarah and John, a couple who were deeply affected by betrayal, find themselves at a crossroads in their relationship in the aftermath of the betrayal. Sarah struggles to trust John again after he was deceived by a former colleague, fearing that he may betray her trust once again. Yet as John demonstrates his commitment to rebuilding trust through his actions and words, Sarah begins to let down her guard and allow herself to be vulnerable with him once again.

As Sarah and John work together to rebuild trust in their relationship, they discover a newfound sense of intimacy and closeness that they had been missing for so long. They learn to communicate openly and honestly with one another, sharing their fears, hopes, and dreams without reservation. Through their shared commitment to rebuilding trust, they forge a deeper connection that strengthens their relationship and binds them together in love and mutual respect.

Another impact of regained trust on personal relationships is the restoration of a sense of security and stability. Betrayal can shake the very foundations of personal relationships, leaving individuals feeling adrift and uncertain about the future. Yet as trust is rebuilt, individuals begin to feel more secure and confident in their relationships, knowing that they can rely on one another to be there through thick and thin.

For example, Emily, a woman who was betrayed by her closest friend, finds herself struggling to trust others in the aftermath of the betrayal. Yet as she begins to rebuild trust in her relationships with her family and loved ones, she discovers a newfound sense of security and stability that she had been missing for so long. She learns to lean on her loved ones for support and guidance, knowing that they will always be there for her no matter what.

As Emily and her loved ones work together to rebuild trust in their relationships, they create a sense of safety and security that allows them to truly thrive. They learn to rely on one another for support and encouragement, knowing that they are stronger together than they are apart. Through their shared commitment to rebuilding trust, they create a sense of belonging and unity that enriches their lives and strengthens their bonds.

In the chapters that follow, we will continue to explore the impact of regained trust on personal relationships, from the restoration of intimacy and closeness to the creation of a sense of security and stability. We will delve into the challenges and triumphs faced by individuals as they navigate the rocky terrain of rebuilding trust in their relationships, and we will examine the broader implications of their journeys for society as a whole. And through it all, we will seek to uncover the seeds of hope and redemption that lie buried within the hearts of individuals, waiting to be nurtured back to life.

Explore the challenges of transitioning from a trustless to a trusting society

Transitioning from a trustless to a trusting society is a complex and multifaceted process that poses a myriad of challenges for individuals and communities alike. After experiencing betrayal and deception, rebuilding trust requires not only individual introspection and growth but also systemic changes in societal attitudes and institutions. In this chapter, we will explore some of the key challenges inherent in this transition and the ways in which characters navigate them on their journey toward rebuilding trust.

One of the primary challenges of transitioning to a trusting society is overcoming deep-seated cynicism and skepticism. In a trustless society, individuals have been conditioned to expect deception and betrayal at every turn, leading to a pervasive sense of cynicism and distrust. Breaking free from this mindset requires individuals to challenge their preconceived notions and beliefs about trust, and to open themselves up to the possibility of vulnerability and connection.

For example, Sarah, a character who has been deeply affected by betrayal, finds herself struggling to trust others in the aftermath of the betrayal. Despite her best efforts to move past her pain and mistrust, she finds herself constantly on guard, wary of being hurt again. It takes time and patience for Sarah to overcome her cynicism and skepticism, and to open herself up to the possibility of trusting others once again.

Another challenge of transitioning to a trusting society is confronting the fear of vulnerability and betrayal. After experiencing betrayal, individuals often erect emotional barriers to protect themselves from being hurt again, making it difficult to open up and trust others. Overcoming this fear requires individuals to confront their past traumas and insecurities, and to take a leap of faith in opening themselves up to others.

For example, Emily, a character who has been betrayed by her closest friend, finds herself struggling to open up and trust others in the aftermath of the betrayal. Despite her desire for connection and intimacy, she finds herself holding back, afraid of being hurt again. It takes courage and resilience for Emily to confront her fear of vulnerability and betrayal, and to take a chance on trusting others once again.

Another challenge of transitioning to a trusting society is navigating the complexities of forgiveness and reconciliation. After experiencing betrayal, individuals often grapple with feelings of anger, resentment, and betrayal, making it difficult to forgive those who have wronged them. Yet forgiveness is essential for healing and moving forward, allowing individuals to let go of their pain and embrace a future built on trust and reconciliation.

For example, John, a character who has been betrayed by his colleagues, finds himself consumed by feelings of anger and resentment in the aftermath of the betrayal. Despite his desire for revenge, he knows that holding onto his anger will only hold him back from healing and moving forward. It takes time and introspection for John to find it in his heart to forgive those who have wronged him, and to embrace a future built on trust and reconciliation.

Yet another challenge of transitioning to a trusting society is confronting the systemic issues and injustices that underlie betrayal and deception. In many cases, betrayal is not simply the result of individual malice or deceit, but is symptomatic of deeper societal issues such as inequality, injustice, and corruption. Addressing these underlying issues requires systemic changes in societal attitudes and institutions, as well as a commitment to social justice and equality for all.

For example, Dr. Maria Chen, a character who has been deeply affected by betrayal, finds herself grappling with the systemic issues and injustices that underlie betrayal and deception. As a computer scientist, she is keenly aware of the ways in which technology can be used to perpetrate acts of deceit and manipulation, and she is determined to use her skills and expertise to address these issues head-on. Through her research and advocacy work, Dr. Chen works to promote transparency, accountability, and social justice in society, laying the groundwork for a future built on trust and equality for all.

Over the course of the upcoming chapters, we will continue to explore the challenges of transitioning from a trustless to a trusting society, from overcoming cynicism and skepticism to confronting the fear of vulnerability and betrayal. We will delve into the personal struggles and triumphs of characters as they navigate these challenges on their journey toward rebuilding trust, and we will examine the broader implications of their efforts for society as a whole. And through it all, we will seek to uncover the seeds of hope and redemption that lie buried within the hearts of individuals, waiting to be nurtured back to life.

Foreshadow conflicts arising from individual struggles during the rebuilding process

As individuals embark on the challenging journey of rebuilding trust in the aftermath of betrayal, they inevitably encounter a myriad of personal struggles and conflicts that threaten to derail their progress. These struggles often arise from deep-seated emotional wounds and insecurities, as well as external pressures and challenges that test their resolve. In this chapter, we will explore some of the conflicts that arise from individual struggles during the rebuilding process and how characters navigate them on their journey toward healing and redemption.

One of the primary conflicts that arises from individual struggles during the rebuilding process is the conflict between forgiveness and revenge. After experiencing betrayal, individuals often grapple with feelings of anger and resentment toward those who have wronged them, making it difficult to let go of their desire for revenge. Yet revenge only perpetuates the cycle of violence and betrayal, further entrenching individuals in a cycle of pain and suffering.

For example, John, a character who has been betrayed by his colleagues, finds himself consumed by feelings of anger and resentment in the aftermath of the betrayal. Despite his desire for revenge, he knows that holding onto his anger will only hold him back from healing and moving forward. Yet letting go of his desire for revenge proves to be a difficult and painful process, as he struggles to find a way to forgive those who have wronged him and move forward with his life.

Another conflict that arises from individual struggles during the rebuilding process is the conflict between self-preservation and vulnerability. After experiencing betrayal, individuals often erect emotional barriers to protect themselves from being hurt again, making it difficult to open up and trust others. Yet true healing and connection can only occur when individuals allow themselves to be vulnerable and open to the possibility of being hurt again.

For example, Emily, a character who has been betrayed by her closest friend, finds herself struggling to open up and trust others in the aftermath of the betrayal. Despite her desire for connection and intimacy, she finds herself holding back, afraid of being hurt again. Yet as she begins to confront her fear of vulnerability and betrayal, she realizes that true healing and connection can only occur when she allows herself to be vulnerable and open to the possibility of being hurt again.

Yet another conflict that arises from individual struggles during the rebuilding process is the conflict between acceptance and resistance. After experiencing betrayal, individuals often struggle to come to terms with the reality of what has happened, clinging to the hope that things will return to how they once were. Yet clinging to the past only prolongs the pain and prevents individuals from moving forward with their lives.

For example, Sarah, a character who has been deeply affected by betrayal, finds herself clinging to the hope that things will return to how they once were in the aftermath of the betrayal. Despite her best efforts to move on and rebuild trust in her relationships, she finds herself resisting the reality of what has happened, unwilling to accept that things have changed. Yet as she confronts her resistance and begins to accept the reality of what has happened, she finds a newfound sense of peace and clarity that allows her to move forward with her life.

Throughout the following chapters, we will continue to explore the conflicts that arise from individual struggles during the rebuilding process, from the conflict between forgiveness and revenge to the conflict between self-preservation and vulnerability. We will delve into the personal struggles and triumphs of characters as they navigate these conflicts on their journey toward healing and redemption, and we will examine the broader implications of their efforts for society as a whole. And through it all, we will seek to uncover the seeds of hope and redemption that lie buried within the hearts of individuals, waiting to be nurtured back to life.

Chapter 5: International Collaborations
Explore collaborations between societies rebuilding trust

In the aftermath of betrayal, societies around the world are confronted with the daunting task of rebuilding trust and fostering transparency in their respective communities. While the journey toward rebuilding trust is often deeply personal and individual, it is also inherently collective, requiring cooperation and collaboration among communities, nations, and societies. In this chapter, we will explore the various ways in which societies come together to collaborate on the shared goal of rebuilding trust, and the impact of these collaborations on the broader process of healing and reconciliation.

One of the primary ways in which societies collaborate on rebuilding trust is through the exchange of knowledge, resources, and expertise. In the wake of betrayal, communities often find themselves grappling with similar challenges and obstacles in their efforts to rebuild trust, from addressing systemic corruption to promoting accountability and transparency. By sharing their experiences and insights with one another, societies can learn from one another's successes and failures, and collectively develop more effective strategies for rebuilding trust.

For example, in the aftermath of a widespread financial scandal, countries from around the world come together to share their experiences and expertise in combating corruption and promoting transparency in the financial sector. Through international conferences, workshops, and forums, representatives from different countries exchange ideas and best practices for holding financial institutions accountable, strengthening regulatory oversight, and promoting ethical behavior in the financial industry. By collaborating in this way, societies are able to learn from one another's experiences and work together to create a more transparent and accountable financial system.

Another way in which societies collaborate on rebuilding trust is through diplomatic efforts and alliances. In the wake of betrayal, countries may find themselves isolated and distrustful of one another, leading to heightened tensions and conflict. By forging diplomatic alliances and partnerships, countries can work together to address common challenges and promote mutual understanding and cooperation.

For example, in the aftermath of a major cyberattack that targets multiple countries simultaneously, governments from around the world come together to coordinate their response and share intelligence on the perpetrators. Through diplomatic channels and international partnerships, countries are able to pool their resources and expertise to track down the perpetrators and hold them accountable for their actions. By collaborating in this way, societies are able to demonstrate their commitment to upholding the rule of law and promoting trust and stability in the international community.

Yet another way in which societies collaborate on rebuilding trust is through cultural exchange and dialogue. In the aftermath of betrayal, communities may find themselves divided along ethnic, religious, or ideological lines, leading to mistrust and hostility between different groups. By fostering cultural exchange and dialogue, societies can break down barriers and build bridges of understanding and empathy between different communities.

For example, in the aftermath of a violent conflict between ethnic groups, communities come together to organize cultural exchange programs and dialogue sessions aimed at promoting reconciliation and understanding. Through these programs, members of different communities have the opportunity to learn about one another's cultures, traditions, and perspectives, and to find common ground and shared values that transcend their differences. By fostering empathy and understanding in this way, societies are able to overcome divisions and rebuild trust among different communities.

In the subsequent chapters, we will continue to explore the collaborations between societies rebuilding trust, from the exchange of knowledge and expertise to diplomatic efforts and cultural exchange. We will delve into the challenges and triumphs of these collaborations, and examine the broader implications of their efforts for the process of healing and reconciliation. And through it all, we will seek to uncover the seeds of hope and redemption that lie buried within the hearts of individuals and societies, waiting to be nurtured back to life.

Characters engage in diplomatic efforts and alliances

In the aftermath of betrayal and the breakdown of trust, characters in our narrative find themselves facing a fractured and distrustful world. Yet amidst the chaos, there arises a glimmer of hope as characters recognize the importance of coming together on an international scale to rebuild trust and foster cooperation. Diplomatic efforts and alliances play a crucial role in this endeavor, serving as vehicles for dialogue, negotiation, and collaboration between nations and societies. In this chapter, we will explore how characters engage in diplomatic efforts and alliances to address the challenges of rebuilding trust on a global scale.

One of the primary ways in which characters engage in diplomatic efforts and alliances is through multilateral organizations and forums. In the wake of betrayal, nations from around the world recognize the need to come together to address common challenges and promote mutual understanding and cooperation. Multilateral organizations such as the United Nations, the World Bank, and the International Monetary Fund serve as platforms for dialogue and collaboration, allowing nations to work together to tackle issues such as corruption, inequality, and conflict.

For example, in response to a global economic crisis triggered by a series of financial scandals, nations from around the world convene at the United Nations to discuss strategies for rebuilding trust and stability in the global economy. Through diplomatic negotiations and dialogue, representatives from different countries work together to develop a coordinated response to the crisis, including measures to strengthen regulatory oversight, promote transparency and accountability, and support economic recovery efforts. By collaborating through multilateral organizations, characters demonstrate their commitment to working together to address common challenges and promote trust and stability in the international community.

Another way in which characters engage in diplomatic efforts and alliances is through bilateral partnerships and agreements. In the aftermath of betrayal, nations recognize the importance of building strong relationships with their allies and neighbors, based on mutual respect, trust, and cooperation. Bilateral partnerships and agreements serve as frameworks for diplomatic engagement, allowing nations to work together to address shared challenges and pursue common interests.

For example, in the aftermath of a major cyberattack that targets multiple countries simultaneously, nations come together to forge bilateral partnerships and agreements aimed at strengthening cybersecurity and defending against future attacks. Through diplomatic channels, governments exchange intelligence, share best practices, and coordinate their response to the threat, demonstrating their commitment to working together to protect their citizens and safeguard the integrity of the global digital infrastructure. By forging bilateral partnerships and agreements, characters demonstrate their willingness to collaborate with their allies and neighbors to address common challenges and promote trust and security in the international community.

Yet another way in which characters engage in diplomatic efforts and alliances is through track-two diplomacy and informal channels of communication. In the aftermath of betrayal, nations recognize the importance of building trust and rapport with their adversaries and rivals, in order to prevent misunderstandings and reduce the risk of conflict. Track-two diplomacy involves unofficial, non-governmental actors such as academics, experts, and civil society organizations, who work behind the scenes to facilitate dialogue and build bridges of understanding between nations.

For example, in the aftermath of a tense standoff between two rival nations, track-two diplomats from both sides come together to organize informal dialogues and meetings aimed at reducing tensions and promoting mutual understanding. Through these informal channels of communication, diplomats are able to engage in frank and open discussions, explore potential areas of cooperation, and build trust and rapport with their counterparts, laying the groundwork for future diplomatic engagement. By engaging in track-two diplomacy, characters demonstrate their commitment to promoting peace, dialogue, and cooperation in the international community.

Across the ensuing chapters, we will continue to explore how characters engage in diplomatic efforts and alliances to address the challenges of rebuilding trust on a global scale. We will delve into the complexities of international diplomacy, from multilateral organizations and bilateral partnerships to track-two diplomacy and informal channels of communication. And through it all, we will seek to uncover the seeds of hope and redemption that lie buried within the hearts of individuals and societies, waiting to be nurtured back to life.

Examine the complexities of rebuilding trust on a global scale

The task of rebuilding trust on a global scale is fraught with complexities and challenges, as nations and societies grapple with the aftermath of betrayal and the erosion of trust in institutions and systems. In this chapter, we will delve into the multifaceted nature of rebuilding trust on a global scale, exploring the various challenges and complexities that arise and the ways in which characters navigate them in their quest for healing and reconciliation.

One of the primary complexities of rebuilding trust on a global scale is the diversity of cultural, political, and social contexts in which trust is understood and experienced. Different societies have different norms, values, and expectations when it comes to trust, making it difficult to develop universal strategies for rebuilding trust that are applicable across all contexts. What works in one society may not necessarily work in another, requiring a nuanced and context-specific approach to rebuilding trust on a global scale.

For example, in some cultures, trust is based on personal relationships and networks of reciprocity, while in others, it is based on formal institutions and systems of governance. In societies where trust has been eroded by corruption and inequality, rebuilding trust may require fundamental changes in the structure and functioning of institutions, while in societies where trust is based on informal networks of trust, rebuilding trust may require fostering stronger interpersonal connections and community bonds. By recognizing the diversity of cultural, political, and social contexts in which trust is understood and experienced, characters can develop more effective strategies for rebuilding trust on a global scale.

Another complexity of rebuilding trust on a global scale is the interconnected nature of modern society, where events and actions in one part of the world can have far-reaching consequences for others. In an interconnected world, issues such as climate change, pandemics, and economic instability require coordinated and collaborative responses from nations and societies, making trust and cooperation essential for addressing shared challenges.

For example, in the aftermath of a global pandemic, nations from around the world come together to develop a coordinated response to the crisis, including measures to contain the spread of the virus, support healthcare systems, and mitigate the economic impact of the pandemic. By working together to address shared challenges, nations demonstrate their commitment to rebuilding trust and cooperation on a global scale, recognizing that no single nation can address these challenges alone. Yet navigating the complexities of global interdependence requires trust and cooperation among nations, as well as a willingness to put aside differences and work together for the common good.

Another complexity of rebuilding trust on a global scale is the legacy of historical injustices and conflicts that continue to shape relations between nations and societies. In many parts of the world, deep-seated resentments and grievances stemming from colonialism, imperialism, and war continue to fuel mistrust and hostility between nations, making it difficult to forge meaningful partnerships and alliances.

For example, in the aftermath of a protracted conflict between two neighboring countries, deep-seated animosities and mistrust continue to hamper efforts to rebuild trust and cooperation on a global scale. Despite repeated attempts at reconciliation and dialogue, both sides remain entrenched in their positions, unwilling to let go of the past and move forward. Yet breaking free from the shackles of history requires courage, empathy, and a willingness to acknowledge past wrongs, as well as a commitment to building a future based on mutual respect and understanding.

In the forthcoming chapters, we will continue to explore the complexities of rebuilding trust on a global scale, from the diversity of cultural, political, and social contexts in which trust is understood and experienced to the interconnected nature of modern society and the legacy of historical injustices and conflicts that continue to shape relations between nations and societies. We will delve into the challenges and complexities of global interdependence, and examine the broader implications of characters' efforts to rebuild trust and cooperation on a global scale. And through it all, we will seek to uncover the seeds of hope and redemption that lie buried within the hearts of individuals and societies, waiting to be nurtured back to life.

Illustrate the echoes of collaboration and unity in the wake of past distrust

In the aftermath of betrayal and distrust, the emergence of collaboration and unity on an international scale serves as a beacon of hope amidst the darkness. Through shared efforts and joint initiatives, nations and societies demonstrate their resilience and determination to overcome past divisions and work together toward a common future. In this chapter, we will explore the echoes of collaboration and unity in the wake of past distrust, highlighting the transformative power of collective action in rebuilding trust and fostering cooperation on a global scale.

One of the most profound echoes of collaboration and unity in the wake of past distrust is the emergence of cross-border partnerships and alliances aimed at addressing shared challenges and promoting mutual prosperity. In an increasingly interconnected world, nations recognize the importance of working together to tackle issues such as climate change, economic inequality, and global pandemics, which transcend national boundaries and require coordinated responses.

For example, in the aftermath of a devastating natural disaster that affects multiple countries, nations from around the world come together to provide humanitarian aid and support to affected communities. Through joint initiatives and collaborative efforts, governments, non-governmental organizations, and international agencies coordinate their response, pooling their resources and expertise to deliver lifesaving assistance and rebuild communities. By working together in this way, nations demonstrate their solidarity and commitment to supporting one another in times of crisis, despite past distrust and animosities.

Another echo of collaboration and unity in the wake of past distrust is the emergence of grassroots movements and civil society initiatives aimed at promoting peace, reconciliation, and social justice. In societies torn apart by conflict and division, ordinary citizens come together to bridge divides, foster dialogue, and build bridges of understanding between different communities.

For example, in the aftermath of a violent conflict between ethnic groups, grassroots organizations and civil society groups work tirelessly to promote reconciliation and healing. Through initiatives such as peace marches, interfaith dialogues, and community reconciliation projects, ordinary citizens from different backgrounds come together to share their stories, confront their shared history, and build trust and understanding. By fostering empathy and solidarity in this way, grassroots movements and civil society initiatives play a crucial role in rebuilding trust and unity in societies torn apart by distrust and division.

Yet another echo of collaboration and unity in the wake of past distrust is the emergence of cultural exchange programs and people-to-people initiatives aimed at fostering mutual understanding and appreciation between different cultures and societies. In an increasingly globalized world, cultural exchange serves as a powerful tool for breaking down barriers, challenging stereotypes, and building bridges of friendship and cooperation.

For example, in the aftermath of a diplomatic crisis between two nations, cultural exchange programs and people-to-people initiatives serve as a means of rebuilding trust and fostering reconciliation. Through initiatives such as student exchange programs, cultural festivals, and artistic collaborations, individuals from different cultures and backgrounds come together to celebrate their shared humanity, transcend their differences, and forge meaningful connections. By promoting cultural exchange in this way, nations demonstrate their commitment to building bridges of understanding and cooperation, despite past distrust and animosities.

Throughout the pages ahead, we will continue to explore the echoes of collaboration and unity in the wake of past distrust, from cross-border partnerships and grassroots movements to cultural exchange programs and people-to-people initiatives. We will delve into the transformative power of collective action in rebuilding trust and fostering cooperation on a global scale, and examine the broader implications of characters' efforts to overcome past divisions and work together toward a common future. And through it all, we will seek to uncover the seeds of hope and redemption that lie buried within the hearts of individuals and societies, waiting to be nurtured back to life.

Chapter 6: The Fragility of Trust Redux
Illustrate the delicate nature of the rebuilt trust

In the aftermath of betrayal and deception, the process of rebuilding trust is a delicate and nuanced endeavor. While characters may succeed in overcoming past traumas and rebuilding trust in their relationships and communities, the fragile nature of this trust is ever-present, vulnerable to the slightest misstep or betrayal. In this chapter, we will explore the delicate nature of the rebuilt trust, examining the ways in which characters navigate the challenges of maintaining trust in the face of uncertainty and vulnerability.

One of the most profound illustrations of the delicate nature of the rebuilt trust is the constant fear of betrayal and deception that lingers in the minds of characters. Despite their best efforts to move on from past traumas and rebuild trust in their relationships, characters find themselves haunted by the fear that history may repeat itself, that those they have come to trust may ultimately betray them once again.

For example, Sarah, a character who has been deeply affected by betrayal in the past, finds herself constantly on edge in her relationships, constantly second-guessing the intentions of those around her. Despite her efforts to trust others and move on from past traumas, she finds herself unable to shake the feeling that she is always one misstep away from being hurt again. The fear of betrayal looms large in her mind, casting a shadow over even the most intimate moments of connection and vulnerability.

Another illustration of the delicate nature of the rebuilt trust is the vulnerability that comes with opening oneself up to others. After experiencing betrayal, characters often erect emotional barriers to protect themselves from being hurt again, making it difficult to fully trust others and open themselves up to vulnerability. Yet true healing and connection can only occur when characters allow themselves to be vulnerable and open to the possibility of being hurt again.

For example, Emily, a character who has been betrayed by her closest friend, finds herself struggling to open up and trust others in the aftermath of the betrayal. Despite her desire for connection and intimacy, she finds herself holding back, afraid of being hurt again. Yet as she begins to confront her fear of vulnerability and betrayal, she realizes that true healing and connection can only occur when she allows herself to be vulnerable and open to the possibility of being hurt again.

Another illustration of the delicate nature of the rebuilt trust is the constant need for reassurance and validation from others. After experiencing betrayal, characters often find themselves seeking constant reassurance from those they have come to trust, seeking validation of their worth and value in the eyes of others. Yet this constant need for reassurance can place a strain on relationships, undermining the very trust they seek to rebuild.

For example, John, a character who has been betrayed by his colleagues, finds himself constantly seeking reassurance from his friends and loved ones, constantly seeking validation of his worth and value in their eyes. Despite their best efforts to reassure him and support him in his healing process, John finds himself unable to shake the feeling of insecurity and doubt that plagues him. The constant need for reassurance drives a wedge between him and those he cares about, undermining the trust and intimacy they seek to cultivate.

In the following sections, we will continue to explore the delicate nature of the rebuilt trust, from the constant fear of betrayal and deception to the vulnerability of opening oneself up to others. We will delve into the challenges of maintaining trust in the face of uncertainty and vulnerability, and examine the broader implications of characters' efforts to navigate these challenges on their journey toward healing and redemption. And through it all, we will seek to uncover the seeds of hope and redemption that lie buried within the hearts of individuals and societies, waiting to be nurtured back to life.

Characters grapple with uncertainties and vulnerabilities

In the aftermath of betrayal and the rebuilding of trust, characters find themselves grappling with uncertainties and vulnerabilities that threaten to undermine the fragile bonds they have worked so hard to rebuild. Despite their best efforts to move forward and leave the past behind, characters are confronted with a myriad of challenges that test their resolve and resilience. In this chapter, we will explore how characters navigate these uncertainties and vulnerabilities on their journey toward healing and redemption.

One of the most profound challenges characters face in the aftermath of betrayal is the uncertainty of the future. After experiencing betrayal, characters often find themselves questioning their beliefs and assumptions about themselves and others, unsure of who they can trust and where they belong. The uncertainty of the future looms large in their minds, casting a shadow over even the most hopeful moments of connection and reconciliation.

For example, Sarah, a character who has been deeply affected by betrayal, finds herself grappling with the uncertainty of the future in the aftermath of the betrayal. Despite her best efforts to move on and rebuild trust in her relationships, she finds herself plagued by doubts and insecurities about what lies ahead. The uncertainty of the future fills her with a sense of unease and apprehension, making it difficult for her to fully embrace the present moment and let go of her fears.

Another challenge characters face in the aftermath of betrayal is the vulnerability that comes with opening oneself up to others. After experiencing betrayal, characters often erect emotional barriers to protect themselves from being hurt again, making it difficult to fully trust others and open themselves up to vulnerability. Yet true healing and connection can only occur when characters allow themselves to be vulnerable and open to the possibility of being hurt again.

For example, Emily, a character who has been betrayed by her closest friend, finds herself struggling to open up and trust others in the aftermath of the betrayal. Despite her desire for connection and intimacy, she finds herself holding back, afraid of being hurt again. Yet as she begins to confront her fear of vulnerability and betrayal, she realizes that true healing and connection can only occur when she allows herself to be vulnerable and open to the possibility of being hurt again.

Another challenge characters face in the aftermath of betrayal is the fear of being hurt again. After experiencing betrayal, characters often find themselves haunted by the fear that history may repeat itself, that those they have come to trust may ultimately betray them once again. The fear of being hurt again looms large in their minds, casting a shadow over even the most intimate moments of connection and vulnerability.

For example, John, a character who has been betrayed by his colleagues, finds himself constantly on edge in his relationships, constantly second-guessing the intentions of those around him. Despite his best efforts to move on and rebuild trust in his relationships, he finds himself unable to shake the feeling that he is always one misstep away from being hurt again. The fear of being hurt again fills him with a sense of anxiety and apprehension, making it difficult for him to fully let go of his fears and embrace the present moment.

Over the upcoming chapters, we will continue to explore how characters navigate the uncertainties and vulnerabilities that arise in the aftermath of betrayal, from the uncertainty of the future to the vulnerability of opening oneself up to others. We will delve into the challenges of overcoming fear and insecurity, and examine the broader implications of characters' efforts to navigate these challenges on their journey toward healing and redemption. And through it all, we will seek to uncover the seeds of hope and redemption that lie buried within the hearts of individuals and societies, waiting to be nurtured back to life.

Explore the challenges of maintaining transparency and trust in the long term

As characters navigate the delicate process of rebuilding trust in the aftermath of betrayal, they are confronted with the daunting task of maintaining transparency and trust in the long term. While initial efforts may lead to a semblance of reconciliation and healing, sustaining trust over time requires ongoing commitment, communication, and vigilance. In this chapter, we will explore the challenges characters face in maintaining transparency and trust in the long term, and the strategies they employ to overcome these challenges.

One of the primary challenges characters face in maintaining transparency and trust in the long term is the temptation to revert to old habits and patterns of behavior. After experiencing betrayal, characters may find themselves falling back into familiar patterns of secrecy, deception, and mistrust, undoing the progress they have made in rebuilding trust.

For example, Sarah, a character who has been deeply affected by betrayal, finds herself struggling to maintain transparency and trust in her relationships in the long term. Despite her initial efforts to open up and rebuild trust with her loved ones, she finds herself reverting to old habits of secrecy and mistrust when faced with challenges or conflicts. The temptation to withhold information or manipulate others to protect herself becomes overwhelming, threatening to unravel the fragile bonds of trust she has worked so hard to rebuild.

Another challenge characters face in maintaining transparency and trust in the long term is the difficulty of addressing underlying issues and conflicts that may arise over time. After experiencing betrayal, characters may find themselves hesitant to confront difficult truths or engage in open and honest communication with others, fearing that doing so may lead to further conflict or betrayal.

For example, Emily, a character who has been betrayed by her closest friend, finds herself struggling to address underlying issues and conflicts in her relationships in the long term. Despite her desire for reconciliation and healing, she finds herself avoiding difficult conversations or sweeping problems under the rug in an attempt to maintain the illusion of harmony and stability. Yet by avoiding conflict and failing to address underlying issues, Emily inadvertently undermines the trust and transparency she seeks to maintain in her relationships, perpetuating a cycle of mistrust and misunderstanding.

Another challenge characters face in maintaining transparency and trust in the long term is the inevitability of change and uncertainty. Over time, relationships evolve, circumstances change, and new challenges arise, presenting characters with new opportunities and obstacles to navigate. Maintaining transparency and trust in the face of change requires adaptability, flexibility, and a willingness to confront challenges head-on.

For example, John, a character who has been betrayed by his colleagues, finds himself grappling with the uncertainty of the future in his professional relationships. Despite his initial efforts to rebuild trust with his colleagues, he finds himself confronted with new challenges and conflicts that threaten to undermine the progress he has made. The uncertainty of the future fills him with a sense of anxiety and apprehension, making it difficult for him to maintain transparency and trust in the long term.

In the chapters ahead, we will continue to explore the challenges characters face in maintaining transparency and trust in the long term, from the temptation to revert to old habits to the difficulty of addressing underlying issues and conflicts. We will delve into the strategies characters employ to overcome these challenges, and examine the broader implications of their efforts to sustain trust and transparency over time. And through it all, we will seek to uncover the seeds of hope and redemption that lie buried within the hearts of individuals and societies, waiting to be nurtured back to life.

Foreshadow potential threats to the fragile trust that has been reconstructed

As characters strive to rebuild trust in the aftermath of betrayal, they are acutely aware of the fragility of the trust they have painstakingly reconstructed. Yet despite their best efforts, the road ahead remains fraught with potential threats and challenges that could unravel the fragile bonds they have worked so hard to rebuild. In this chapter, we will explore the potential threats to the fragile trust that has been reconstructed, foreshadowing the obstacles characters will face on their journey toward healing and redemption.

One of the most significant potential threats to the fragile trust that has been reconstructed is the possibility of betrayal from within. Despite their best intentions, characters may find themselves tempted to betray the trust of those they care about in pursuit of their own interests or desires. Whether out of fear, insecurity, or selfishness, characters may succumb to the temptation to deceive or manipulate others, jeopardizing the trust and stability they have worked so hard to build.

For example, Sarah, a character who has been deeply affected by betrayal, finds herself tempted to betray the trust of her loved ones in the aftermath of a personal crisis. Despite her initial efforts to rebuild trust and repair her relationships, she finds herself overwhelmed by fear and insecurity, leading her to make choices that ultimately undermine the fragile bonds of trust she has worked so hard to rebuild. The possibility of betrayal from within looms large in her mind, casting a shadow over even the most intimate moments of connection and vulnerability.

Another potential threat to the fragile trust that has been reconstructed is the influence of external forces and factors beyond characters' control. Whether in the form of societal pressures, political turmoil, or economic instability, external forces can pose a significant threat to the trust and stability of characters' relationships and communities. In the face of uncertainty and upheaval, characters may find themselves torn between competing loyalties and obligations, leading to conflicts and tensions that strain the fragile bonds of trust they have worked so hard to build.

For example, Emily, a character who has been betrayed by her closest friend, finds herself caught in the crossfire of a bitter dispute between rival factions in her community. Despite her desire to remain neutral and impartial, she finds herself pressured to take sides and choose between loyalty to her friends and loyalty to her community. The influence of external forces and factors threatens to undermine the fragile trust and stability of her relationships, leaving her torn between competing loyalties and obligations.

Yet another potential threat to the fragile trust that has been reconstructed is the possibility of unforeseen events and circumstances that disrupt characters' lives and relationships. Whether in the form of natural disasters, personal tragedies, or unexpected betrayals, unforeseen events can shake characters' faith in themselves and others, testing the resilience of the fragile bonds of trust they have worked so hard to build.

For example, John, a character who has been betrayed by his colleagues, finds himself facing unexpected challenges and setbacks in his professional and personal life. Despite his best efforts to move on from past traumas and rebuild trust in his relationships, he finds himself blindsided by a series of unforeseen events that threaten to undo the progress he has made. The possibility of unforeseen events and circumstances shakes his faith in himself and others, leaving him questioning whether the fragile bonds of trust he has reconstructed can withstand the trials and tribulations that lie ahead.

As we progress through the chapters, we will continue to explore the potential threats to the fragile trust that has been reconstructed, from the possibility of betrayal from within to the influence of external forces and factors beyond characters' control. We will delve into the ways in which characters navigate these threats and challenges, and examine the broader implications of their efforts to sustain trust and stability in the face of uncertainty and adversity. And through it all, we will seek to uncover the seeds of hope and redemption that lie buried within the hearts of individuals and societies, waiting to be nurtured back to life.

Chapter 7: The Crossroads of Hope

Characters stand at the crossroads of hope and uncertainty

In the final chapter of our journey, characters find themselves standing at the crossroads of hope and uncertainty, facing pivotal decisions that will shape the future of their relationships, their communities, and their world. As they confront the challenges and trials that lie ahead, characters must draw upon their courage, resilience, and determination to navigate the uncertainties of the path before them and embrace the hope that lies on the horizon.

One of the most profound moments in which characters stand at the crossroads of hope and uncertainty is when they are faced with the choice to trust again. After experiencing betrayal and deception, characters must decide whether to open their hearts to the possibility of being hurt again or to close themselves off from the world in fear and mistrust. In this moment of reckoning, characters must confront their deepest fears and insecurities, and find the strength within themselves to take a leap of faith into the unknown.

For example, Sarah, a character who has been deeply affected by betrayal, finds herself standing at the crossroads of hope and uncertainty as she contemplates whether to trust again in her relationships. Despite her past traumas and the fear that history may repeat itself, Sarah realizes that she cannot continue to live her life in fear and mistrust. With courage and determination, she chooses to open her heart to the possibility of being hurt again, embracing the hope that lies on the other side of her fears.

Another moment in which characters stand at the crossroads of hope and uncertainty is when they are faced with the choice to forgive those who have wronged them. After experiencing betrayal and deception, characters must decide whether to hold onto their anger and resentment or to let go of the past and embrace forgiveness. In this moment of truth, characters must confront the pain and hurt that lies within their hearts, and find the compassion within themselves to forgive those who have wronged them.

For example, Emily, a character who has been betrayed by her closest friend, finds herself standing at the crossroads of hope and uncertainty as she contemplates whether to forgive those who have wronged her. Despite the pain and hurt she has endured, Emily realizes that holding onto her anger and resentment will only perpetuate the cycle of betrayal and mistrust. With courage and compassion, she chooses to let go of the past and embrace forgiveness, knowing that it is the only way to truly heal and move forward.

Yet another moment in which characters stand at the crossroads of hope and uncertainty is when they are faced with the choice to rebuild trust and reconciliation in their relationships. After experiencing betrayal and deception, characters must decide whether to take a chance on rebuilding the bonds of trust and connection with those they care about or to walk away and start anew. In this moment of reflection, characters must confront their deepest desires and fears, and find the courage within themselves to take the first step toward healing and reconciliation.

For example, John, a character who has been betrayed by his colleagues, finds himself standing at the crossroads of hope and uncertainty as he contemplates whether to rebuild trust and reconciliation in his professional relationships. Despite the pain and betrayal he has endured, John realizes that walking away from his colleagues will not erase the hurt and mistrust that lies within his heart. With courage and determination, he chooses to take a chance on rebuilding the bonds of trust and connection, knowing that it is the only way to truly heal and move forward.

In the chapters that follow, we will continue to explore the moments in which characters stand at the crossroads of hope and uncertainty, facing pivotal decisions that will shape the future of their relationships, their communities, and their world. We will delve into the challenges and trials that lie ahead, and examine the transformative power of hope and resilience in the face of adversity. And through it all, we will seek to uncover the seeds of hope and redemption that lie buried within the hearts of individuals and societies, waiting to be nurtured back to life.

Explore the decisions that will shape the future

As characters stand at the crossroads of hope and uncertainty, they are faced with a myriad of decisions that will shape the future of their relationships, their communities, and their world. These decisions are not made lightly, as they carry the weight of past traumas and the hope for a better tomorrow. In this pivotal moment, characters must draw upon their strength, resilience, and wisdom to make choices that will lead them toward healing, reconciliation, and redemption.

One of the most significant decisions characters must make is whether to confront the past or to let it go and move forward. After experiencing betrayal and deception, characters are often haunted by the ghosts of their past, unable to fully embrace the present or envision a future free from the shadows of the past. In this moment of truth, characters must confront their deepest fears and insecurities, and find the courage within themselves to let go of the past and embrace the possibilities of the future.

For example, Sarah, a character who has been deeply affected by betrayal, finds herself at a crossroads as she contemplates whether to confront the past or to let it go and move forward. Despite her desire for closure and resolution, Sarah realizes that holding onto the past will only perpetuate her pain and suffering. With courage and determination, she chooses to let go of the past and embrace the possibilities of the future, knowing that it is the only way to truly heal and move forward.

Another significant decision characters must make is whether to trust again or to close themselves off from the world in fear and mistrust. After experiencing betrayal and deception, characters are often hesitant to open their hearts to the possibility of being hurt again, fearing that history may repeat itself. In this moment of reckoning, characters must confront their deepest fears and insecurities, and find the strength within themselves to take a leap of faith into the unknown.

For example, Emily, a character who has been betrayed by her closest friend, finds herself at a crossroads as she contemplates whether to trust again or to close herself off from the world in fear and mistrust. Despite her past traumas and the fear that history may repeat itself, Emily realizes that closing herself off from others will only perpetuate her pain and isolation. With courage and determination, she chooses to open her heart to the possibility of being hurt again, knowing that it is the only way to truly heal and move forward.

Yet another significant decision characters must make is whether to forgive those who have wronged them or to hold onto their anger and resentment. After experiencing betrayal and deception, characters are often consumed by feelings of anger, bitterness, and resentment toward those who have wronged them. In this moment of truth, characters must confront their deepest wounds and insecurities, and find the compassion within themselves to forgive those who have hurt them.

For example, John, a character who has been betrayed by his colleagues, finds himself at a crossroads as he contemplates whether to forgive those who have wronged him or to hold onto his anger and resentment. Despite his past traumas and the pain he has endured, John realizes that holding onto his anger will only perpetuate the cycle of betrayal and mistrust. With courage and compassion, he chooses to forgive those who have wronged him, knowing that it is the only way to truly heal and move forward.

Throughout the pages ahead, we will continue to explore the decisions that will shape the future of characters' relationships, communities, and world. We will delve into the challenges and trials that lie ahead, and examine the transformative power of hope, resilience, and redemption in the face of adversity. And through it all, we will seek to uncover the seeds of hope and redemption that lie buried within the hearts of individuals and societies, waiting to be nurtured back to life.

Examine the choices individuals and society must make to secure a trusting future

As characters stand at the crossroads of hope and uncertainty, they are confronted with choices that will not only shape their own futures but also the future of their communities and society as a whole. These choices are laden with significance, as they have the power to either perpetuate the cycle of mistrust and betrayal or pave the way for healing, reconciliation, and a more trusting future. In this pivotal moment, characters must grapple with the weight of their decisions and find the courage to chart a path forward toward a brighter tomorrow.

One of the most significant choices individuals and society must make to secure a trusting future is the choice to prioritize transparency and accountability in all aspects of life. After experiencing betrayal and deception, individuals and society are often left reeling from the consequences of unchecked power and corruption. In this moment of reckoning, individuals and society must confront the need for greater transparency and accountability in their institutions, relationships, and interactions, and take decisive action to hold those in positions of power accountable for their actions.

For example, Sarah, a character who has been deeply affected by betrayal, finds herself at a crossroads as she contemplates the importance of transparency and accountability in her personal and professional relationships. Despite her past traumas and the fear that history may repeat itself, Sarah realizes that the only way to truly rebuild trust and ensure a more trusting future is to prioritize transparency and accountability in all aspects of her life. With courage and determination, she chooses to hold herself and others accountable for their actions, knowing that it is the only way to break free from the cycle of mistrust and betrayal.

Another significant choice individuals and society must make to secure a trusting future is the choice to foster empathy, compassion, and understanding in their interactions with others. After experiencing betrayal and deception, individuals and society are often left grappling with feelings of anger, resentment, and mistrust toward those who have wronged them. In this moment of truth, individuals and society must confront the need for greater empathy, compassion, and understanding in their relationships and interactions, and take intentional steps to heal the wounds of the past and build bridges of connection and reconciliation.

For example, Emily, a character who has been betrayed by her closest friend, finds herself at a crossroads as she contemplates the importance of empathy and understanding in her relationships with others. Despite her past traumas and the pain she has endured, Emily realizes that the only way to truly move forward and create a more trusting future is to foster empathy, compassion, and understanding in her interactions with others. With courage and determination, she chooses to extend grace and forgiveness to those who have wronged her, knowing that it is the only way to break free from the cycle of hurt and betrayal.

Yet another significant choice individuals and society must make to secure a trusting future is the choice to actively participate in the rebuilding and strengthening of their communities. After experiencing betrayal and deception, individuals and society are often left feeling disconnected and isolated from one another. In this moment of reflection, individuals and society must confront the need for greater solidarity, cooperation, and collaboration in their communities, and take proactive steps to rebuild trust, foster unity, and create a sense of belonging for all members of society.

For example, John, a character who has been betrayed by his colleagues, finds himself at a crossroads as he contemplates the importance of community and solidarity in his professional life. Despite his past traumas and the challenges he has faced, John realizes that the only way to truly heal and create a more trusting future is to actively participate in the rebuilding and strengthening of his community. With courage and determination, he chooses to reach out to his colleagues, mend broken relationships, and work together toward a shared vision of a more trusting and inclusive workplace.

In the chapters that follow, we will continue to explore the choices individuals and society must make to secure a trusting future, from prioritizing transparency and accountability to fostering empathy and understanding, and actively participating in the rebuilding and strengthening of their communities. We will delve into the challenges and trials that lie ahead, and examine the transformative power of hope, resilience, and redemption in the face of adversity. And through it all, we will seek to uncover the seeds of hope and redemption that lie buried within the hearts of individuals and societies, waiting to be nurtured back to life.

Set the stage for the series conclusion

As we reach the final chapter of our journey, the crossroads of hope and uncertainty loom large before our characters. They have faced trials and tribulations, navigated through the depths of betrayal and mistrust, and emerged on the other side with hearts full of resilience and courage. Now, as they stand at the precipice of the unknown, they are faced with a choice: to succumb to fear and despair or to embrace the hope that lies within them and forge a path toward redemption.

Throughout our journey, we have witnessed the transformative power of hope and resilience in the face of adversity. We have seen characters rise above their past traumas and reclaim their agency, their dignity, and their sense of purpose. We have seen communities come together in solidarity and compassion, standing shoulder to shoulder in the face of seemingly insurmountable challenges. And through it all, we have seen the seeds of hope and redemption take root in the hearts of individuals and societies, guiding them toward a brighter tomorrow.

As we set the stage for the series conclusion, it is important to reflect on the lessons we have learned and the journey we have undertaken together. We have explored the myriad ways in which trust can be shattered and rebuilt, the complexities of human nature and society, and the enduring power of resilience, compassion, and forgiveness. We have delved into the depths of despair and emerged on the other side with a newfound sense of hope and possibility.

Now, as we stand on the threshold of the series conclusion, it is time to bring our journey to its ultimate culmination. It is time to witness the final chapters of our characters' stories, to see how their choices and actions will shape the future of their world, and to discover whether redemption and reconciliation are truly within reach. It is time to bid farewell to the characters we have come to know and love, and to celebrate the triumph of the human spirit in the face of adversity.

But even as we prepare to say goodbye, let us remember that the journey does not end here. The lessons we have learned, the bonds we have forged, and the hope we have kindled will continue to guide us on our own journeys long after the final page has been turned. And as we carry these lessons with us into the future, let us take solace in the knowledge that no matter how dark the night may seem, the dawn of a new day is always just beyond the horizon.

In the chapters ahead, we will witness the culmination of our characters' journeys, as they confront their fears, embrace their hopes, and chart a course toward a brighter future. We will see how their choices and actions will shape the world around them, and we will discover whether the seeds of hope and redemption that have been planted in their hearts will ultimately blossom into a future filled with promise and possibility. And through it all, we will celebrate the indomitable human spirit and the enduring power of hope to light the way through even the darkest of times.

Conclusion

Summarize key events and developments in "Rebuilding Trust"

Throughout our journey in "Rebuilding Trust," we have witnessed a tapestry of events and developments that have shaped the lives of our characters and the world they inhabit. From the ashes of betrayal and mistrust, they have risen, forging new connections, confronting old wounds, and striving to rebuild the fractured bonds of trust that bind them together. As we reflect on the key events and developments that have unfolded, we are reminded of the resilience of the human spirit and the transformative power of hope in the face of adversity.

At the heart of our story lies the aftermath of betrayal, as our characters grapple with the devastating consequences of shattered trust. We have witnessed the emotional toll it takes on individuals and society, as they struggle to come to terms with the betrayal of those they once trusted implicitly. We have seen how betrayal fractures relationships, undermines institutions, and leaves a trail of devastation in its wake. But amidst the wreckage, we have also seen the seeds of renewal take root, as characters confront their pain and begin the journey toward healing and redemption.

As our characters embark on the journey of rebuilding trust, we have witnessed the collective healing process unfold, as communities come together to support one another in the aftermath of betrayal. We have seen the importance of transparency and accountability in rebuilding trust, as characters strive to create a more open and honest society. We have witnessed the triumphs and challenges of the rebuilding process, as characters navigate personal transitions and confront the uncertainties of a trustless world.

In our exploration of technological redemption, we have seen characters strive to redeem technology's role in trust, as they harness innovation and safeguards to regain faith in the systems that govern their lives. We have examined the ethical considerations inherent in the technological rebuilding process, as characters grapple with the moral implications of their actions and strive to ensure that technology serves the greater good.

As characters navigate the complexities of rebuilding trust on a global scale, we have seen the echoes of collaboration and unity in the wake of past distrust. We have witnessed the power of international collaborations, as characters engage in diplomatic efforts and alliances to rebuild trust between societies. We have explored the fragility of trust in the face of uncertainty, as characters confront the challenges of maintaining transparency and trust in the long term.

In our exploration of the fragile nature of trust, we have seen characters grapple with uncertainties and vulnerabilities, as they confront the potential threats that loom on the horizon. We have examined the challenges of maintaining transparency and trust in the long term, as characters strive to safeguard the fragile bonds they have worked so hard to rebuild. And we have foreshadowed potential threats to the fragile trust that has been reconstructed, as characters stand at the crossroads of hope and uncertainty, facing pivotal decisions that will shape the future of their world.

As we reach the series conclusion, we are reminded of the resilience of the human spirit and the enduring power of hope to light the way through even the darkest of times. We have witnessed the transformative journey of our characters, as they confront their fears, embrace their hopes, and chart a course toward a brighter future. And as we bid farewell to the characters we have come to know and love, we carry with us the lessons they have taught us and the hope they have inspired. For in the end, it is not the darkness that defines us, but the light that we carry within us, guiding us on our journey toward redemption and renewal.

Reflect on the collective and individual journeys of rebuilding

As we come to the conclusion of our exploration in "Rebuilding Trust," it is essential to take a moment to reflect on the collective and individual journeys that have unfolded throughout our narrative. From the initial devastation of betrayal to the eventual triumph of resilience and hope, our characters have navigated a tumultuous path toward redemption, each facing their own trials and tribulations along the way.

At the heart of our story lies the collective journey of rebuilding trust within society as a whole. We have witnessed the profound impact of betrayal on communities, institutions, and relationships, as trust is shattered and bonds are broken. But amidst the wreckage, we have also seen the resilience of the human spirit, as individuals come together to support one another in the aftermath of betrayal. Through acts of kindness, compassion, and solidarity, communities begin the process of healing, laying the groundwork for a more trusting future.

Individually, our characters have embarked on their own journeys of rebuilding, each confronting their own demons and striving to find redemption in the face of adversity. We have seen characters grapple with the emotional toll of betrayal, as they struggle to come to terms with the loss of trust and the pain of deception. We have witnessed their courage and determination as they confront their fears, confront their fears, and take the first steps toward healing and renewal.

Throughout their journeys, our characters have faced a myriad of challenges, from navigating personal transitions to grappling with uncertainties and vulnerabilities. We have seen them confront the complexities of rebuilding trust on a global scale, as they navigate diplomatic efforts and alliances to rebuild trust between societies. We have watched as they strive to redeem technology's role in trust, harnessing innovation and safeguards to regain faith in the systems that govern their lives.

But amidst the challenges and trials, we have also seen moments of triumph and resilience, as our characters rise above their past traumas and embrace the hope that lies within them. We have seen them forge new connections, mend broken relationships, and rebuild the bonds of trust that bind them together. And through it all, we have seen the transformative power of hope, resilience, and forgiveness in the face of adversity.

As we reflect on the collective and individual journeys of rebuilding, we are reminded of the resilience of the human spirit and the enduring power of hope to light the way through even the darkest of times. We have witnessed the transformative journey of our characters, as they confront their fears, embrace their hopes, and chart a course toward a brighter future. And as we bid farewell to the characters we have come to know and love, we carry with us the lessons they have taught us and the hope they have inspired.

In the end, "Rebuilding Trust" is not just a story of betrayal and redemption, but a testament to the resilience of the human spirit and the capacity for forgiveness and renewal. It is a reminder that even in the face of seemingly insurmountable challenges, there is always hope for a better tomorrow. And as we carry these lessons with us into the future, let us remember that trust, once broken, can be rebuilt, and that the journey toward redemption is always worth the effort.

Pose thought-provoking questions about the future of trust in the series' conclusion

As we conclude our journey through "Rebuilding Trust," we are left with lingering questions about the future of trust in our world. The trials and triumphs of our characters have provided us with valuable insights into the complexities of trust, the fragility of human relationships, and the enduring power of resilience and hope. But as we look to the future, we must confront the uncertainties and challenges that lie ahead, and ask ourselves thought-provoking questions about the nature of trust and its role in shaping our world.

One question that arises is: How do we rebuild trust in a world that has been shattered by betrayal and deception? Throughout our narrative, we have seen characters grapple with this question, as they confront the devastating consequences of broken trust and strive to find redemption in its wake. But as they embark on the journey of rebuilding, they must confront the challenges of rebuilding trust in a society that has been fractured by mistrust and suspicion. How do we heal the wounds of the past and forge new connections that are built on a foundation of trust and mutual respect? This question challenges us to consider the steps we must take to rebuild trust in our own lives and communities, and to confront the barriers that stand in the way of reconciliation and renewal.

Another question that arises is: What role does transparency and accountability play in rebuilding trust? Throughout our narrative, we have seen characters grapple with the importance of transparency and accountability in rebuilding trust, as they strive to create a more open and honest society. But as they confront the challenges of holding themselves and others accountable for their actions, they must confront the complexities of balancing transparency with privacy, and accountability with forgiveness. How do we create systems and institutions that are transparent and accountable, without sacrificing the privacy and autonomy of individuals? This question challenges us to consider the delicate balance between transparency and accountability, and to find ways to hold ourselves and others accountable for our actions, while also respecting our fundamental rights and freedoms.

A third question that arises is: How do we navigate the complexities of rebuilding trust on a global scale? Throughout our narrative, we have seen characters grapple with the challenges of rebuilding trust between societies, as they navigate diplomatic efforts and alliances to bridge the divide between nations. But as they confront the complexities of cultural differences and historical grievances, they must confront the question of how to foster collaboration and cooperation in a world that is increasingly polarized and divided. How do we build bridges of trust and understanding between nations, and work together toward a common vision of peace and prosperity? This question challenges us to confront the barriers that stand in the way of international cooperation and to find ways to build trust and solidarity across borders.

A fourth question that arises is: What role does technology play in shaping the future of trust? Throughout our narrative, we have seen characters grapple with the ethical implications of technology, as they strive to redeem its role in trust and rebuild faith in the systems that govern their lives. But as they confront the challenges of balancing innovation with accountability, they must confront the question of how to harness the power of technology for the greater good, while also safeguarding against its potential for abuse and manipulation. How do we ensure that technology serves the needs of society, rather than the interests of a select few? This question challenges us to consider the ethical implications of technological development and to find ways to ensure that technology is used as a force for positive change in our world.

As we ponder these thought-provoking questions about the future of trust, we are reminded of the complexity and nuance of the human experience. Trust is not a static concept, but rather a dynamic and evolving process that requires constant attention and care. And as we look to the future, we must confront the uncertainties and challenges that lie ahead, and work together to build a world that is grounded in trust, integrity, and mutual respect. For in the end, trust is the foundation upon which all human relationships are built, and it is only by nurturing and protecting this foundation that we can create a future that is worthy of our highest aspirations.

THE END

Glossary

Here are some key terms and definitions related to AI-driven cryptocurrency investing:

1. Trust: The firm belief in the reliability, truth, or ability of someone or something.

2. Redemption: The action of saving or being saved from sin, error, or evil.

3. Echoes: Repetition or imitation of a sound produced by reflection of sound waves.

4. World: The earth, together with all of its countries, peoples, and natural features.

5. Striving: Making great efforts to achieve or obtain something.

6. Mend: Repair or restore something that is broken or damaged.

7. Fabric of Trust: The interconnected network of relationships and institutions built on mutual reliance, honesty, and reliability.

Potential References

In addition to the content presented in this book, we have compiled a list of supplementary materials that can provide further insights and information on the topics covered. These resources include books, articles, websites, and other materials that were used as references throughout the writing process. We encourage you to explore these materials to deepen your understanding and continue your learning journey. Below is a list of the supplementary materials organized by chapter/topic for your convenience.

Introduction:

Duhigg, Charles. "The Power of Habit: Why We Do What We Do in Life and Business." Random House, 2012.

Brown, Brené. "Daring Greatly: How the Courage to Be Vulnerable Transforms the Way We Live, Love, Parent, and Lead." Avery, 2012.

Chapter 1: Aftermath of Betrayal:

Baumeister, Roy F., and Mark R. Leary. "The Need to Belong: Desire for Interpersonal Attachments as a Fundamental Human Motivation." Psychological Bulletin, vol. 117, no. 3, 1995, pp. 497-529.

Kramer, Roderick M., and Tom R. Tyler. "Trust in Organizations: Frontiers of Theory and Research." Sage Publications, 1996.

Chapter 2: Societal Healing:

Putnam, Robert D. "Bowling Alone: The Collapse and Revival of American Community." Simon & Schuster, 2000.

Fukuyama, Francis. "Trust: The Social Virtues and the Creation of Prosperity." Free Press, 1995.

Chapter 3: Technological Redemption:

Floridi, Luciano. "The Fourth Revolution: How the Infosphere is Reshaping Human Reality." Oxford University Press, 2014.

Johnson, Steven. "Future Perfect: The Case for Progress in a Networked Age." Riverhead Books, 2012.

Chapter 4: Individuals in Transition:

Heath, Chip, and Dan Heath. "Switch: How to Change Things When Change is Hard." Crown Business, 2010.

Seligman, Martin E.P. "Learned Optimism: How to Change Your Mind and Your Life." Vintage Books, 1998.

Chapter 5: International Collaborations:

Fukuyama, Francis. "Identity: The Demand for Dignity and the Politics of Resentment." Farrar, Straus and Giroux, 2018.

Pinker, Steven. "Enlightenment Now: The Case for Reason, Science, Humanism, and Progress." Viking, 2018.

Chapter 6: The Fragility of Trust Redux:

Giddens, Anthony. "The Consequences of Modernity." Stanford University Press, 1990.

Beck, Ulrich. "Risk Society: Towards a New Modernity." Sage Publications, 1992.

Chapter 7: The Crossroads of Hope:

Diamond, Jared. "Collapse: How Societies Choose to Fail or Succeed." Penguin Books, 2005.

Harari, Yuval Noah. "21 Lessons for the 21st Century." Spiegel & Grau, 2018.

Conclusion:

Pinker, Steven. "The Better Angels of Our Nature: Why Violence Has Declined." Viking, 2011.

Csikszentmihalyi, Mihaly. "Flow: The Psychology of Optimal Experience." Harper Perennial, 1990.

www.ingramcontent.com/pod-product-compliance
Lightning Source LLC
Chambersburg PA
CBHW072105040426

42334CB00042B/2490